S0-EDK-714

ALONG *The* **California** WINE TRAIL

"Do not go where the path may lead,
go instead where there is no path and leave a trail."

– Ralph Waldo Emerson

WRITTEN BY **JERRY STROUD**
PAINTINGS BY **KERNE ERICKSON**

GREG YOUNG PUBLISHING, INC.
P.O. Box 2487
SANTA BARBARA, CALIFORNIA 93120
www.gregyoungpublishing.com
e-mail: greg@gregyoungpublishing.com

1st Edition

Written by Jerry Stroud
e-mail: script434@aol.com • www.alongthecaliforniawinetrailauthor.com

Artwork by Kerne Erickson

Layout and design by Jennifer Pechette
e-mail: jennpechette@gmail.com

Printed in Hong Kong by Integrated Communications • www.icla.com

ISBN: 978-0-692-93807-2
Library of Congress Control Number: 2017953971

californiawinetrail.com

FOREWORD

Every bottle of wine tells a story. And behind those stories, there are often generations of families whose lives are shaped by the magic of the grape and the challenge to create something spectacular. This is true for me, as it is for many of the wine country pioneers you'll read about in this book.

I first fell in love with Paso Robles while I was at UC Davis in the Enology program. There were seventeen of us. At that time, Napa and Sonoma were already far ahead in the industry of making premium wines. Paso Robles was in its infancy (I became the fifth winery there) but I fell in love. My professors promised me this would be a great wine region. I believed them and I wasn't alone. Efforts from people like Herman Schwartz, Vic Roberts, Tom Martin and Jerry Lohr also helped put Paso, and Paso wines, on the map.

I remember those early years being filled with a lot of hard work and a lot of fun. But my story is not unique. With every wine appellation in California, there are pioneers who pave the way. Even though today's wine industry is far different from the one I started out with, we're all making great wines but facing different challenges, technologies and regulations that we must work with. What matters most is a love of the land, the soul of a winemaker, and the perseverance to succeed.

When I started out in 1973, we were blazing a trail because we knew in our hearts that California would become one of the finest wine regions in the world. New generations may choose to follow our course or forge their own path in this industry. Either way, I can attest that California creates some of the best wine in the world. All you have to do is open a bottle to find out.

Cheers,
Gary Eberle

ALONG
The
California
WINE TRAIL®

MENDOCINO
ANDERSON VALLEY
CLEAR LAKE
CALISTOGA
DRY CREEK VALLEY
ST. HELENA
RUTHERFORD
SACRAMENTO
EL DORADO
FAIR PLAY
CALIFORNIA SHENANDOAH VALLEY
ALEXANDER VALLEY
OAKVILLE STAGS LEAF DISTRICT
NAPA VALLEY
FIPPLETOWN
SONOMA VALLEY
FORT ROSS SEAVIEW
RUSSIAN RIVER VALLEY
SAN FRANCISCO
LODI
AMADOR
SIERRA FOOTHILLS
NORTH COAST
LIVERMORE VALLEY

CARMEL VALLEY
MONTEREY
SANTA LUCIA HIGHLANDS
ARROYO SECO
CENTRAL VALLEY
MADERA
FRESNO
CENTRAL COAST
PASO ROBLES
EDNA VALLEY
ARROYO GRANDE VALLEY
BALLARD CANYON
SANTA MARIA VALLEY
SANTA YNEZ VALLEY
STA RITA HILLS
HAPPY CANYON OF SANTA BARBARA
MALIBU COAST
CUCAMONGA VALLEY
LOS ANGELES
SANTA CATALINA
TEMECULA VALLEY
SALTON SEA
SOUTH COAST
SAN DIEGO

Pacific Ocean

N
W E
S

DRAWING BY SCOTT WESTMORELAND
© GREG YOUNG PUBLISHING, INC.

4

TABLE OF CONTENTS

PUBLISHER'S NOTE

My journey down this trail began in early 2011. Winemaker Geoff Rusack and I were having a discussion regarding the Ballard Canyon area in the Santa Ynez Valley of Santa Barbara County. Geoff was defining Ballard Canyon's unique climate and topography, which produces world-class Rhone varietals. While we discussed this, I had a thought... how can I assist Geoff with helping create more awareness to Ballard Canyon, a very unique and beautiful place, that is not often traveled and few people are aware of? It was during this conversation I started thinking of a concept to accomplish this. The initial idea of promoting awareness to one specific wine-producing region, quickly grew into a statewide project. I soon realized my endeavor to promote California's American Viticulture Areas would be no easy task, since there are well over one hundred in California. I thought to myself, what better way of introducing people to California's AVAs than a story told by writer Jerry Stroud and paintings by artist Kerne Erickson? The journey down this trail has been met with enthusiasm from everyone that I have encountered.

I'd like to thank Jonathan Walters– Chair of Lake County Wine Grape Growers Commission and Director of Farming for Brassfield Estate Winery– for his time, sharing of his great knowledge, and the suggestion that we experience the marvelous sunrise over Clear Lake. We spent that entire day touring and exploring Clear Lake sub-AVAs– I will always remember and appreciate the experience and Jonathan's natural enthusiasm.

I am truly appreciative and grateful for the creative efforts of writer Jerry Stroud and editor/designer Jennifer Pechette, whose endless patience and hard work made this book a reality. And to Gordon McClelland– thank you for introducing Kerne Erickson, whose paintings are like windows, providing the viewer a taste of the awesome bounties that the wine trail has to offer. Thank you Kerne, for your creativity, endless hours and dedication to the project.

Thank you to my dear wife Ashley and my children Jozef and Mia, for their support, patience, and love. They are the "Bright Stars" in my life.

There are so many other individuals that made invaluable contributions, I cannot express my gratitude enough. *Thank you!* The completion of this book– this joyful and wonderful feat– could not have happened without each and every one of your efforts.

Greg Young
President, Greg Young Publishing, Inc.
Santa Barbara, California

ACKNOWLEDGMENTS

The immediate attraction to author *Along the California Wine Trail* was based upon several ideals. California was home. Wine was a shared joy. And to express words that compliment Kernes nostalgic paintings was a paring that resonated with me. The concept was fresh– something untold. A wise man once said, "Opportunity has one hair on its head. When it passes by you've gotta' grab it."

So, I did.

And while I put on hold the lost Oceanic art of a man whose story will be told another day, the decision was based upon a desire to pursue a journey that was, at its very core, my own. It was a trail I had lived, whose ranchers and farmers I had grown up with, whose countryside I had wandered through. To share stories of those lives who have helped transform this complex world of winemaking, in places I still call home, became deeply personal.

And who more passionate a man to champion California's viticultural story than Greg Young? It was Greg's vision, his ability to communicate and inspire with crushing perseverance that was paramount to the book coming to fruition. The growers' stories and vineyard images would not have graced these pages if not for this gentleman publisher.

My sincere thanks go out to the book's editor and layout designer Jennifer Pechette whose page turning notes were both invaluable and inspiring– her lay out structure, and fresh design added a creative element to the book that beautifully compliments the words and paintings throughout these pages

Thanks to my beautiful wife, Suzanne, whose patience at home was unending, and whose companionship on the road allowed us more time together as we experienced California's delicious rewards along the way.

My thanks go out to Kerne Erickson. Having the privilege to share words alongside his buttery soft and alluring paintings is a paring, more than I could have hoped for.

With that said, my sincerest thanks go out to those of you who shared your time and stories with me as I traveled the open road. Your lives touched me in ways I did not expect. So, as the book reflects by the nuances of color and expression California's beautiful "sense of place," so does it reflect the best of individuals themselves– and to you, I'm truly grateful.

Jerry Stroud
Author

SIERRA FOOTHILLS

— AMERICAN VITICULTURAL AREA —

THE SIERRA FOOTHILLS
American Viticultural Area

"They say we're gonna' have an inch of rain tomorrow," Dick Cooper, owner of Cooper Vineyards says as we drive slowly by a block of Barbera– his Lab Blondie by his side. Dick is looking toward the vineyard with his signature cowboy hat shading his brow. I don't quite know if he's talking to me or to the vines passing by, reassuring them that it's gonna' be okay.

This is how ruthlessly dry the season had been in California. His remarks also reflect how he, and many other foothill grape growers, are connected to their vineyards. His appreciation and attention to their temperament and personality is as genuine as his smile. He can't hide the fact that this ever growing relationship between man and vineyard is born by family ties– generations of them– and whether tapestried in October colors or bud breaking naked in spring, they speak to him. Dick is not alone in his respect for the foothill vineyards, or belief in those wines born by them. In speaking with others from the Shenandoah Valley, like winemaker Joe Shebl of Renwood Winery, vineyard manager Tony Sanchez at Sobon Winery, and owner Andy Friedlander of Andis Wines, there is a movement going on. Not only is the Shenandoah Valley producing award winning wine with their signature Zinfandel and bold Barbara, but planted acreage throughout the region is at an all time high. Grape growers are coming to the foothills because place matters— they are introducing new varietals that are favorable to the region.

It is a renaissance defined by change that has led to a broader swath of Rhône varietal plantings. Grapes like Rousanne, Mourvèdre, Grenache, and Marsanne are thriving. Well known varietals like Syrah and Viognier are bringing character to blended reds— adding diversity to wines for those enthusiast seeking something more. Established wines like Sangiovese, Barbera and Primitivo are increasing in production, along with more signature wines predominant to the foothills like Zinfandel and Cabernet Sauvignon. The foothills are on the move! And despite the recent seasons of drought, the vintages have been impressive and the region continues its march forward.

Since the foothills resurrection in the seventies, planted acreage has increased by the thousands; yet with this ascent, the region has not reached the pinnacle of respect it deserves.

The five sub-appellations within the Sierra Foothills AVA— El Dorado, Fair Play, Fiddletown, Shenandoah Valley, and North Yuba— have been slow to maturation. There has been little notice to the region's viticultural significance, some referring to the Sierra Foothills as having "sub par viticulture." In Andrew Friedlander's words regarding their assessment... "It's been tough."

Despite this, the vision for the future is unwavering, and speaks of the growers and vintners commitment and belief in what lies ahead. They have their tastings, winemaker dinners, and vintner associations leading marketing efforts; they host wine festivals like Amador County's *Big Crush* with nearly 5000 attendees in celebration of the grape harvest... all of this toasting the region's success.

"The foothills are on the move!"

The altitude and character of the Sierra Foothills speak of a higher calling. The soil is consistently composed of volcanic loam above 1500 feet, with sandy loam of predominately decomposed granite below this level. The terra-cotta colored iron top soil is visible at almost every cut bank. The depth of the soil is minimal, varying from inches to several feet and is considered by many viticulturists as having great suitability for Rhône varieties. Though much of the land is unsuitable for planting vineyards, growers from across the country are coming to this immense AVA with great aspirations— there remain thousands of acres of valleys, rolling hills, and steeped mountainsides suitable for growing a host of varietals. The Sierra Foothill AVA covers seven counties and encompasses 2.6 million acres— 5,800 of this planted vineyards. There are over 125 wineries. Those looking to bring new character to the bottle are turning to this affordable, virtually untapped region.

The terroir can best be described by Jeff Meyers, General Manager at Terra d'Oro Winery, who refers to the foothill region as having a "Mediterranean climate" seen in Old World countries. Like Spain and Italy, a vast number of its micro climates are consistently

CALIFORNIA

SHENANDOAH

V·A·L·L·E·Y

— AMERICAN VITICULTURAL AREA —

K·ERICKSON

higher, brighter, and steeper than other wine regions in the state. The foothills begin at five hundred feet and climb to three thousand feet towards a clear sky– rising above the noise and industrial lees of pollution that often settle in valley floors. The foothills reside closest to the grand Sierra Nevada mountain range to the east. These mountains form a wall that stretches north to south for approximately 400 miles. From Fredonyer Pass to Tehachapi pass, Pacific storms have stacked up on its western side and blasted the face of the Sierra Nevada's for eons. It was exposure to these countless storms that eventually decayed the mountains to form the up and down character, vast array of soils, and micro climates that make up today's Sierra Foothills.

Here, the region draws breath from down drafting alpine winds and warm upward winds from the valley floor. The variety of trees that thrive in the high altitude sun are natural born filters. The winds offer a whispering of fragrances... notes of pine needle, blooming buckeye and tannin scented oak. The foothills have a consistent climate with mostly warm days and cool nights. The region may encounter several days of fog and a dusting or two of snow per year, but it is the morning frost at bud break that the vineyards are most vulnerable– the damning chill with its dagger like follicles can smother a vineyard in minutes. Not so much in the northern appellations like Fairplay or El Dorado where forest tree cover and steeper terrain shelter the vine, but in the open unprotected lands throughout Amador County like Shenandoah Valley and Fiddletown. Here you will see wind machines scattered throughout the open vineyards.

"The winds offer a whispering of fragrances... notes of pine needle, blooming buckeye and tannin scented oak."

These towering sentinels stand guard over the vines, helping to raise temperatures in an effort to protect their tender shoots.

Later that morning, Dick Cooper points out some irregularities in a straw field beyond the vineyards. "See that?" he asks, "It's from early miners. They were great hydraulogists." The miners certainly traveled far and worked hard– Dick respects that– and I didn't press the grievances I have regarding the early miners. Unlike many, my own understanding of the era is a period in California history that pilfered the very "sense of place" that is at the heart of the vineyard...the land.

It's easy to understand the lore and why the legacy continues. It's easy to fall into romantic trappings as dreams of riches called to the vast number of immigrants who traveled here. It's also easy, as a self-proclaimed "historian," to see how their transgressions were not only systematically sugar coated with lore, but as muddied with falsehoods as hydraulic dredging.

During the late eighteen hundreds, many unsuccessful gold prospectors turned to grape growing and winemaking, only to find themselves under siege– their once "fellow" gold seeking immigrants now burrowing beneath their vineyards. The hydraulic techniques used by miners were a clear and blatant threat. The farmers were at arms with them and due to this atrocity— a law was passed in 1884 banning hydraulic mining, protecting farmers from the invasive wrath ravaging the earth beneath their feet.

More importantly, foothill farmers were practicing sustainability before they knew the significance attached to it. They were the Uptons, Ulhingers, Deavers and the D'Agostinis whose families respectfully pioneered Shenandoah Valley in the mid 1800's; the Sobons who were handed the torch from the D'Agostinis in 1989 and have carried the light of responsible farming into the era of sustainable practice.

Today they are professional growers like Andrew Friedlander, whom I had the pleasure of meeting— an educated man whose "green" Andis winery and wines are a mark of environmental and architectural excellence. They are vintners that encourage visitors from across the country to view the area, educating them to the importance of what's happening here. They are families inviting guests to share in the abundance of foothill wines, pouring glasses in tasting rooms throughout the region. They welcome the traveler onto their property. In fact, you will be hard pressed to find a more amicable, approachable community than the Sierra Foothills.

There are the new generation of wine growers as well, transcending the formidable past with the promise of tomorrow. This progress is not made due to any sense of snobbery or elitism. It is made by a breathing, living co-existence with the land, the animals and the communities we share our world with.

History tells us the miners brought the first vines to the foothills in the Coarse Gold Gulch area. That was in the mid 1800's and is historically significant. These were early settlers— immigrants who planted vineyards and established cottage wineries. By the late eighteen hundreds the region was saturated with as many as one hundred wineries during its crescendo. The Possessory Act in 1852 allowed the foothill farmers to file for ownership of the land and patent acres of land for farming— land they would eventually call home. This encouraged farming and was good reason to begin the endeavor of planting vines. And plant they did... the Sierra Foothills is said to have been the most prolific wine growing region in the state during this era!

By building houses and planting vineyards the farmers discovered their own sense of place here— one that would last for generations. They planted more than vines, they planted family roots to the land. They understood the importance of environment and the significance of conservation. It is what established the wine growers' place in the foothills— a fit between land, varietal and people. This sense of "oneness" inevitably caused the wine industry's growth. It was not thoughts of nuggets dancing in their heads. They came with a plan and that plan came progressively. It was this plan, decades later, that inevitably led to the greatest boom— the wine growing bump in the 1970's. Crop demand skyrocketed, and the value of foothill grapes were recognized for their intensity, spice, and fruit packed boldness.

The miners abandonment and personal indifference to the Sierra foothills impacted

"Foothill grapes were recognized for their intensity, spice, and fruit packed boldness."

the future of the wine industry immensely. People saw the region as done. There was nothing left to mine and perception during these difficult times influenced indifference. Then came the Great War– the Volstead Act in 1919, the collapse of the mines in the 1920's, the great depression, the stock market crash, and eventually the second world war– it was an industry punished by circumstance. The economic wrath had produced the perfect storm. And even though prohibition was repealed in 1933, it wasn't grapes that were sought out for planting, but walnut and prune orchards. Grape interest in the region was literally crushed– pressed back decades by uncontrollable events due in part to the gold rush collapse.

Yet, there continues in today's Sierra Foothills an unavoidable association with wine and gold. Jingles like "the hills are filled with grape gold," or "the new gold rush of the Sierras", or "liquid gold." The old cliches continue throughout the region. I understand the legacy.

The bread and butter of the wine industry's past begins with its own history, and no better a place to rip a chunk of bread from its remarkable past than at Sobon Estate's museum– one of few wineries who continued producing wine through prohibition. Their story speaks of tireless generations before them, responsible individuals prospering in communion with the land and each other.

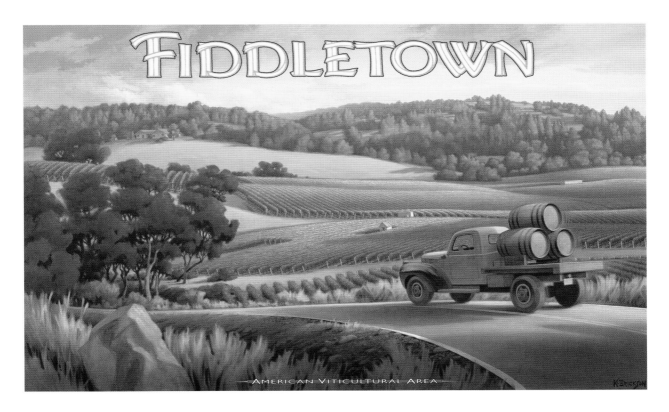

FIDDLETOWN

— AMERICAN VITICULTURAL AREA —

In the cellar's museum are old vats, tools and equipment that once pressed the fruit and worked the fields, and images of pioneering men who worked the land. These are the remarkable stories of responsible individuals who closed deals with a handshake.

I'm a history guy. California's my home and mining is its legacy. It will forever remain an important piece of California's architecture. But to continue chirping about the miners association with wine is a colossal mis-pairing. The blend sours the taste buds and waters my eyes just thinking of it. In fact, if I hear another "Strike it rich in the Sierra Foothills" in reference to wine, or the "New Gold Frontier" as a simile for the region by local rags, brochures or newspapers– that's it! I'll drive straight to Jackson, find a saloon, and get hammered on some cheap southern whiskey.

There are blogs talking about the foothills providing wine for thirsty miners during the gold rush, and there is no question they did, but the term "thirsty" for the miner in relation to wine is a stretch. I'm not talking about toothless immigrants in cranky saloons sniffing Zinfandel from granite ware mugs, grumbling about buttery notes and burping up sourdough biscuits. Most of these guys worked in and around water all day– it came with the job. So they had plenty of time to quench their thirst and mend their pruning toes. But quenching thirst with wine? The majority of miners were a hardcore bunch of drinkers whose incessant need for alcohol and all night benders certainly wasn't quenched by wine as much as it was by whiskey and other hard core spirits that packed a snort and swallow. The best bang for the coin came with a drink that taunted law and tortured livers.

I understand the gold rush jingle provides traffic to hotels, shops and the general community. Traffic means dollars and dollars make sense. The gold miners legacy continues just as the hotels of the era continue to thrive with their stacked brick walls, creaky porch walkways, tin overhangs and antique consignment shops enticing travelers like myself to step in. They should. It's a rich, genuine story ideally built for tourism as well as a great snapshot to California's rowdy past. It's foothill history. I get it, but the Sierra Foothills are producing award wining wines. Today's pioneering individuals are expanding its footprint beyond the wine clubs, local markets and tasting rooms. Travelers to the foothills are raising their glasses to the region's success– filling their preceptors with the complexity of an aromatic pairing. The alpine and ponderosa scented air paired with a fruity bold Barbera, resonates with this delicious sense of place. This is where the wine enthusiast can indulge in arguably some of the finest Zinfandel in the state– at stellar tasting rooms with stunning vistas.

This is the allure of the Sierra Foothill AVA... its wine. The foothills are more than just gold country with a "sidekick." Wine country is the story here, and the promise is what's happening now– today. The region's continued diversity in planted grapes is transforming varietal life near the mountain tops. But the silence here is deafening and is one of the challenges facing the Sierra Foothills. There's need for noise.

Sure, the tranquility here is sublime and its charm unforgettable. The feeling of "awayness" is part of its attraction and unquestionably a source of its viticultural appeal, but the foothills need to be heard... people need to get here... it needs to be seen. Yet its footprint takes us off the four lane freeway. *OMG!* It leads us away from the cherished Apple Stores, pop culture coffee houses and beyond that "fifty miles and I won't eat sushi" threshold. These are conveniences the pampered public bathe in. Even locals will tell you the drive home is a "poke" from any major city– out of the way for some, too far for others.

> ## "There's need for noise. The foothills need to be heard... people need to get here... it needs to be seen."

However, the road travelled today is changing. It is one of the many reasons the foothills is growing. Attention to highways and country roads have transformed immensely, and with today's automobiles– their safety, mileage improvements and technological advancements– is there really any inconvenience? I thought my parents' 60 Ford station wagon was space age stuff with its ultra cool rear power window. Today we have social network, satellite radio, and a host of other advancements imbedded in our cars. It doesn't matter if you're driving the coast highway along those snaking roads or doing the ups and downs between Napa and Sonoma or Lake County. Today's vehicle allows the traveler unparalleled riding comfort even on the most challenging roads. They are living rooms on wheels; space age technologically driven devices steering their

own wheels for God's sake. What else does the pampered traveler need? When driving from the valley floor to the foothills, it's as calming as if I'd just turned onto the last road home. My greatest challenge is fighting off a nap. It's that comfortable.

As I leave the mass traffic through Central Valley, pass Lodi and traverse the first incline heading towards the Sierra Foothills, I take a breath, immediately knowing the craziness is behind me. I'm closer now to my destination– that place away from the busyness city life stacks on me. I find the road up here simple and calming. The drive so visibly appealing I'd pay to travel it. In fact, having lived in Orange County I'm surprised there are no toll roads charging me to get there. It's that beautiful.

So, if you're looking for a memorable drive this is it. More importantly, if you're a wine enthusiast seeking a higher calling, there is no better time than now to pop a cork, experience the delicious character of foothill wines and make some noise!

Further into the morning Dick points to a healthy block of Barbera, "My father told me, 'Son,'" Dick smiles, "'don't ever plant here. It's too gravelly.'" Then he chuckles respectfully, pleased at the sight of the healthy Barbera vines having overcome the odds– not gloating over success in the face of his father's advice, but proud of the vines flourishing in the face of diversity. It is this determination– that sense of "gut feeling" that farmers like Dick have for their crops– that leads to a closer connection to the vineyards. One that is in many ways paternal– a rare instinct born by sheer affection for the

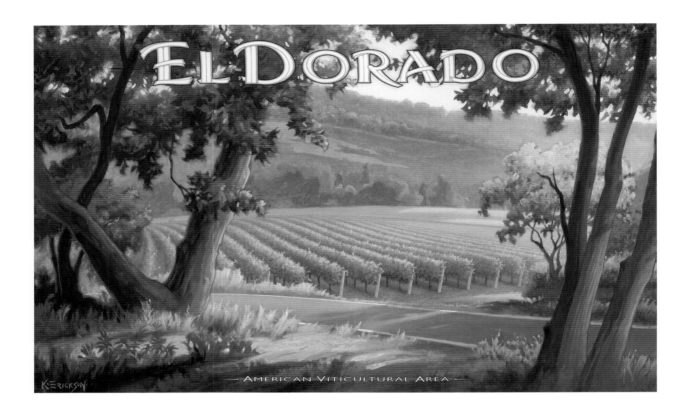

ELDORADO

— AMERICAN VITICULTURAL AREA —

vineyard and experience with the land. It isn't science. It isn't book talk. It's less of a business to the farmer than it is a fulfilling lifestyle. It's years of a life dedicated to caring for this sense of place and for the vines who've found their home here.

From North Yuba County to Mariposa County, foothill farmers like Dick Cooper have a vision of sustainable farming. A new green is happening. It is more than talk– sustainable, natural, organic, and biodynamic practices have been adopted by the grape grower. Many grape growers have their own philosophies regarding these practices. Dick Cooper doesn't subscribe to organic farming. He believes it has no more benefit to the environment or community than the prevailing practice of sustainability– responsible attention to the ecology. He, like many, understand the community's own sense of place within the farm. The five thousand dollars worth of bird netting he purchased is rolled up in the barn. He prefers planting rows of bird feeders along chosen spots to keep the migrating birds from ravaging the grapes. The predators are doing well with rodent control. He uses his farmed sheep manure for fertilizer. He dry farms and cultivates alternating rows. There are as many variations in farming practices today as there are wines to choose from– and they are as diverse as the wines themselves.

I asked Jeff Meyers about biodynamic farming... "Yeah, I know about it." He, like many, regard it without much fan fair. The reality is, biodynamic is only a fraction of today's farming practice. Wineries are reluctant to cross over usually because they don't believe in biodynamic, or to transform their farming practices to meet the strict requirements can be extremely challenging.

It's a paramount risk for any grape grower, especially the established. It's not like adopting sustainable practice where you address crop cover, go solar, change to biodiesel, or fabricate bird houses for predators to control rodents. With biodynamic farming you're picking crops by the stars, pruning vineyards by the planets, and burning mice pelts by the dozens. That's right, actually torching them to be sprayed into the air upon the vineyard. Sure these things are at the far end of the practice spectrum, but to be "Demeter Certified" these standards do apply. It is changing a winery's entire growing philosophy; implementing something as ideological as a palm reader into the house and leaving everything you've invested to the Wine Gods. And the truth is, wineries like Terra d'Oro have worked tirelessly to get to where they are. Things are working in the foothills.

Certainly tradition is meant to be challenged. Like Dick Cooper whose respect for his father's beliefs were successfully challenged in the vineyards, it should come as no revelation that change is imminent today. Farming practices will inevitably transcend today's methods as they will transcend tomorrow's— it is the beauty of the industry. This isn't a tale about new, but the story of old. It's been evolving for centuries and will continue to do so at the behest of another generation seeking non traditional methods themselves. The demand is happening today.

The wines produced in the foothills have many renditions to their story. Those of a classic traditional wine, like the foothill's signature Zinfandel, are similar to a classic

Shakespeare story— having a good number of interpretations with nuance, personality and human influence distinctly their own. Whether these wine "stories" are characterized by terroir or cellar influence, some will continue to please us, others not.

And among the vineyard blocks and tilled rows, a growing number of other stories are waiting patiently to be told. They may pale in comparison to their peers but they are scattered among the foothill acres waiting for the vintners hand to bring them some measure of prominence. They are the "other wines" yearning to be understood and talked about for who they are. The Millennial generation will be the deciders of tomorrow's wines. They will champion those grapes that bring another character to the bottle.

As every new wine tells its own story, so does the foothill winemaker whose influence in the cellar creates a personal rendition of them. Whether its cold fermentation, organic, new French barrels or American oak— cellar influence is growing in the foothills. The winemaker's craft can compliment or break the story.

North Yuba is the smallest sub appellation in the foothills. It consists of 30 square miles with less than a dozen wineries in its region, while its neighboring El Dorado sub appellation has over 60 wineries. Within the southern area of the El Dorado AVA sits the Fair Play AVA— close to 20 wineries are located amongst its twisting turns and mountain-top terroir.

At the heart of the Sierra Foothills, in the county of Amador, lies two other sub-appellations that complete the Sierra Foothills

AVA: the Shenandoah Valley AVA and its adjacent Fiddletown AVA. Here you will find over 50 wineries and a plethora of other unique experieces, one of these being the refreshing enclave in Plymouth called Amador 360. Though it has no scenic view, its "360 degree view" jingle of lesser known Amador wines is an experience worth tasting. You'll be introduced to wines produced by unknown makers, part time viticulturists, as well as established winemakers with their own foothill brand. Just around the corner you will find Taste restaurant featuring an exquisite menu, a fine wine list and a cast of professionals that could've came straight from a five star Metropolitan restaurant. It is the "go to" place for local and out of town wine professionals.

The local wines talked about are many. Some prominent, others not. They consist of a cornucopia of varietals, enough Old World names to tongue tie even the most educated Rosetta Stone enthusiast– over thirty varietals from Spain to Italy being grown throughout the appellations. They are reds like Albariño, Vermantino, Fiano, Verdelho, Mouvedere, Greco di Tufo, and white varietals from France's Rhône valley like Roussanne, Marsanne, Viognier and more.

The "crunchy wines" with high alcohol levels and what Robert Parker refers to as "Hedonistic fruit bombs," are prominent in the foothills. They will continue to be championed, while a movement towards Rhône and Burgundy varietals of a more elegant note is concurrently changing the viticultural landscape in the foothills. And that change is happening today.

That boring sameness among many present day wines is why diversity will overcome similarity. This is the Sierra Foothills' sweet spot. It will not come tomorrow. It will not come with a smash, bang or immediate celebration. It will come gradually– day by day, year by year– and this movement will eventually transform the industry. It will be led by today's generation, and generations who follow– individuals who are not only in search of their own identity but who seek to define themselves and their pleasures by those elements enhancing their daily lives.

Later that day Dick says, "I'm sorry about kidnapping you for so long. I just like driving around my vineyards. I like looking at them." It was a telling statement. Like a great wine there was complexity to what influenced those words. "Looking at," defined by the grape grower, is not something visible to those of us unfamiliar with this paternal connection they share. What the farmer "sees" comes with age. It comes with experience and is drawn from the countless struggles and triumphs born by them. In Dick Cooper's case, three generations of them.

As we "putted" between the vineyards at a tractor's pace in the comfort of his truck and best friend Blondie, I could see he was in his element– able to express so eloquently in words the deep respect he had for these vineyards that have consumed him; explaining how his wines came to be and how years caring for them helped to define himself. Just hearing him speak of their company seemed to soothe him. His own words validated generations that have looked over this place. The "putt" through the vineyards was a giving of thanks to family and to the land he so

"What the farmer 'sees' comes with age.
It comes with experience and is drawn from the
countless struggles and triumphs born by them."

loved. It was no wonder he "just" liked looking at them. They spoke to him. It was as if he was somewhere else in far better company than I when he talked of them. The more he reminisced, the further back he traveled. The years came seamlessly to him. He was now in a time prior to the vineyards when his grandfather farmed hay— fuel for horses who powered the carriages.

While these early days working the hay fields were met with great challenges, the farmers were able to overcome them. It was this longevity and wisdom that earned them a respectable place in the foothills. To this day, there is no belly aching, no whining, no resentment brought on by hardship, only solutions to them. Some work. Some don't. The lines drawn in their leathered skin and solid handshakes reflect their toil and resolve. It's that simple. They continue working, tirelessly seeking better ways— knowing well the importance of tomorrow.

The fact that some of the oldest Zinfandel vines in the world come from the Sierra Foothills is reason to talk about them. Those gnarly vines with their flaking skins and strapping arms are testament to the region's viability and rootstock grit. Vineyards estimated to be planted as late as the 1840's in the Coarse Gold Gulch area appear to flourish with the wears of age. They go back generations, many vineyards outliving the very lives that brought them here— a compliment to every grower.

Jeff Meyers believes there's a good possibility all foothill Zinfandel clones come from original Deaver rootstock— the vines providing an invaluable source for clonal selection from these noble Foothill patriarchs. In fact, there is a profound sense of celebration of "old" throughout the foothill region as well as the wine industry itself. While ageism is an issue throughout much of corporate America, here in the wine industry, old is embraced! At the very heart of old age abounds a true sense of spirit. It is genuine. Old denotes a silver lining. Think of the old farmer, the old vine vineyards and the old wine. Old is as valued and refreshing as a bud breaking spring. When one views the old vines among the foothills and tastes the character their grapes deliver, its reverence is understood.

Today, the "Grandpere Vineyard" in the Shenandoah Valley is a fitting example. The 143 year old vines planted by John and Mary Upton on a gentle slope of foothill land, continue to produce high quality wines. Equally impressive are the crops harvested by Terra d'Oro Winery from the Deavers' 140 year old Zinfandel vines. These are ancient hipster vines with decades of torrential rainstorm parties and ground shaking earthquakes beneath their roots. They are the "rock stars" of every region's envy and one that brings celebrity status with it. The word "old," when referencing vineyards, has not only a a sense of celebrity attachment to it, but a soulful spirit is implied to the vineyards as well as to the wine. The label sells bottles. It is in many ways an agricultural darling. Where else in today's society will old experience that kind of love?

When asked about what threshold legally determines old in regards to the vines, Jeff Meyers just laughed. "Three years old can be considered old." How's that for a slippery slope? I have iPhones older than that.

Yet, these 143 year old "Ancestor Vines" on this 14 acre piece of Amador County land is testament to the foothills triumph. They are the region's legacy. They speak of wisdom. Their rootstock provides big brother cloning to those existing young vines that one day will become ancestor vines themselves.

The following morning a rainstorm blew in to the Sierra Foothills just as Dick Cooper had promised. It crept in early to the pleasure of many. I stepped onto the Historic Imperial Hotel's balcony to look over the grey wet past. If history had a face this was it– Amador City, the heart of generations born and gone. Old was preserved everywhere. The tin roofs, porch over hangs and clunky boardwalks resonated with dirt from the past.

Looking over Main Street I understood the importance of California's history. It was at the heart of the town's legacy, and yet, the Sierra Foothills has respectfully outgrown its historic gone by years. More fittingly, the region is now a slice of wine country's future– and like a farmer's old pair of jeans, it is the perfect fit.

While the morning rains continued to drench the city's hardscape, I was reminded how

deeply needed a good drenching was to the region. Looking over this antiquated town, I thought of those pioneering grape growers who had to care for their parched and thirsty vineyards without technological advancements.

"These ancient vines are the "rock stars" of every region's envy."

Their struggles brought on by drought, pestilence and other hardships were unending. But "back in the day" history tells us the vineyards thrived. There were no drip systems, no sprinklers, no pagers beeping vineyard managers that frost was imminent. There were no pads to tap or apps to assist, no weather Doppler to inform them, and more importantly, no dead batteries to charge.

There was only the "Farmer's Almanac." It was the go to reference book for every farmer. Nothing more. The fact is, it is still Mother Earth who decides what the day will bring. Ultimately the sun, climate and soil is what determines life among the foothills and the outcome of every vintage. This is the farmer's sustenance as well... earth. It is what they depend on. Without her benevolence, all of mankind's crops would be withered and render even the best technological advancements passé.

Grape growers know the importance of the environment. Their awareness is nurturing a better understanding of those things tied to earth. They are wrapping their minds around

FAIR PLAY

— AMERICAN VITICULTURAL AREA —

K. ERICKSON

responsible farming practices, and by doing so, are cultivating the importance of tomorrow. It was good to see the Sierra Foothill vineyards in the care of these responsible farmers– generations of them whose confidence in the region's future is to this day unwavering.

While leaving Amador wine country, I felt like I was driving away from a dear old friend. I had learned something more than is simply taught or seen among the vineyards; there was a sense of place here. The fresh drafting alpine air with its soft frangances of oak, pine and buckeye, delivered without condition.

To share in the company born by these natural elements was to be entranced by a place you'll find no where else. Is it any wonder the word Amador means "one who loves?"

As I drove home the rain continued to fall. It was good to see the fields drinking and the gullies swelling. The vineyards bathed by the rain seemed to have a sense of celebration to them. Harvest was in, and even though it had come two weeks early, it surely pleased the farmer who had cause to celebrate. I envisioned growers and vintners raising glasses at dinner tables across the foothills, giving thanks to this gloomy wet grey presence. It wasn't much, but it was a start– helping water tables to rise, assisting leaves to color and fall, and allowing vineyards exhausted by the year's challenging drought to rest in preparation for the coming year.

I thought of that sun drenched morning with Dick Cooper, his elbow hanging out the open window, not knowing if he was talking to me or to the vines, but knowing this... there was more to his words than a promise that rain would come.

RUSSIAN RIVER VALLEY

AMERICAN VITICULTURAL AREA

THE NORTH COAST
American Viticultural Area

"If you drive through Napa, you pass castles. Drive through the Russian River Valley and you pass barns." This was the owner of Toad Hollow Vineyards, Frankie Williams, expressing with a sense of pride the wine regions cultural differences. And it's clear. The Russian River Valley today resembles a place I could have easily driven through decades ago. Its charm is as timeless and valued by those who live here as the faux castles and grand chateaus are to those who reside along Napa Valley's Silverado Trail.

The Russian River Valley is one of many sub appellations within the North Coast AVA. It is an acclaimed growing region whose wines like Pinot Noir and Chardonnay thrive in its coveted soils.

A short walk from Frankie Williams' vineyards, along Westside road, is a block of vineyard that looks as plain as any other-- rolling hills in the backdrop, oak groves, straw blonde hillsides— yet this is no common block of vineyard, but one that helped bring spectacular to a bottle and revolutionized the wine industry in California; a vineyard that helped define the North Coast region's wine as the best in the world.

This is Bacigalupi Vineyards whose contribution of grapes sourced to Chateau Montelena helped win the West. It took a blind tasting "across the pond" to come to the realization by its French peers, whose wines have for centuries defined best in class, that The New World, and specifically Napa County's Chateau Montelena's 1973 Chardonnay, would outclass their own to become legendary.

Titled "The Judgment of Paris," Time magazine's foreign correspondent George Taber broke the news of the May 24, 1976 results. Taber's four paragraph story was at the time considered "filler," today it is hailed "as the greatest news story ever written about wine."

The Burgundian terroir so chirped about by French enophiles was suddenly second class. British wine merchant Steven Spurrier's attempt at bringing California wine to light by placing New World wines in a Paris blind tasting, surprisingly trumped the French wines. The infamous high scoring white wine had come from Napa's Chateau Montelena, a 1973 Chardonnay produced by master winemaker Milejenko Grgich.

It was a seminal moment in wine history. But if the grapes contributed to the Napa Chateau Montelena wine really didn't come from Napa, should it matter? What if the distinct soil, the micro climate, the elevation that help to define character and personality in this particular vintage had come from another appellation? Several in fact. What if, in reality a percentage of the grapes had been sourced mountains away from the Napa Valley in a viticultural area designated as the Russian River Valley— in a modest block of vineyard owned and managed by Charles and Helen Bacigalupi?

I had the pleasure of sitting down with 90 year old Matriarch Helen Bacigalupi on a foggy morning at the winery's tasting room. Her husband Charles had passed away in 2013. Beside Helen was her granddaughter Nicole, who along with her parents and twin sister Katherine, have taken over the reins to the Bacigalupi Vineyards.

Helen, a sharp witted, business savvy woman recalled the day Mike Grgich called her from Chateau Montelena saying, "Did you hear? Your grapes were used in the Chardonnay that won the Judgment." There was a proud sense of accomplishment to her smile. I asked Helen if the Paris Judgement changed the course of her and Charles' winery as it had for those others involved in its success? If it brought acclaim to them? "Not so much." said Helen. "It did though, make Mike Grgich rich," and "put California on the map." She laughs, shrugging off the respect gleaned upon all those involved with the Judgement but her. After all they were only grapes. They were only a large percentage of two other Sonoma County grapes used in the making of the 1973 Napa labelled vintage.

After my interview, Lee Hodo, a local wine marketing expert with 36 years experience, and currently representing the Bacigalupi family, drove us to the block of vineyards near Helen's home that contributed to the seminal event. The vineyards appeared unremarkable. Yet, if they could speak they would tell another story... that it was they who helped give birth to the 1973 Chardonnay vintage that Chateau Montelena purchased, that Mike Grgich had cellared, and that inevitably found its way to the infamous tasting in Paris.

I picked up some vineyard soil and ran it between my fingers. The earth was warm and crumbly. Harvest had come early. The pregnant bunches bulging from the vines had been delivered weeks earlier, and the remnant grapes left to hang were now measurably sweetened by summers end. Giving birth was reflected throughout this block of seemingly forgotten vineyard. Days of green had passed, the vines appeared exhausted. It was time for a season of rest. The dormant sleeping days of fall and winter were ahead, until another year of warming begins the vines' journey— a season of growing that one day might give birth to another spectacular vintage to be remembered by.

Before leaving the Russian River Valley, I had the privilege of lunching with Frankie Williams at Wily's in Healdsburg. Frankie, a Blythe Danner look alike, expressed her joy and passion for the business after having taken over the winery in 2007. Her late husband Todd, had passed away unexpectedly, leaving her to carry on a legacy that continues today.

Frankie shared with me some candid thoughts on the industry... The business is a "jungle" out there. The people are "a joy." The competition is "huge."

When I asked Frankie what she was most proud of, there was no hesitation. It was her ability to carry on with the winery— to continue what Todd had left behind— a desire to provide fine wine at affordable prices.

She said a wine critic once remarked, "Frankie, you'll never get the respect your wines deserve at these prices." She laughed. There wasn't disappointment or regret. In fact for Frankie, there was a sense of satisfaction in what concerned the critic. That was the mission Todd had championed since inception– affordable prices! And this approachable and much appreciated journey continues today– classy, delicious, whimsically branded wines that more people can enjoy.

> "This approachable and much appreciated journey continues today– classy, delicious, whimsically branded wines that more people can enjoy.

All too often the experts, the wine critics and marketers attach dollars to bottles. But the Toad Hollow story was never about pleasing those dollar dishing chumps who cackle about how much they spent on a bottle. Everyone knows there are good wines, great wines, and occasionally wines we use to goose the drain with. High prices for some are justified– rarity, vintage, best in class will always command respectable prices. They should. Scoring is another pricing influenced matter.

It is one of the few irony's that follow the business of wine– that one must pay mightily to consume what is best. For many, drinkability has become a price influenced matter. The idea that taste is greater if you pay more is a wine fallacy based on consumer mind set. The critic who spoke of "respect" regarding Toad Hollow wine was referring to cost and sale ability, not taste. It was a reference to consumer perception and not the wines' quality– not a note about its personality or

the influence of its terroir, but a price tag glued to the bottle.

The more than one hundred thousand cases Toad Hollow has distributed across the country is a tribute to Todd and Frankie's story; a success story based upon a model of affordability, fun, and quality without price tag worries. It is a legacy that continues today and is shared at the Toad Hollow tasting room centered in the town of Healdsburg.

Outside of Healdsburg, west of Highway 101, is the Dry Creek Valley– a stretch of road as rural today as it was nearly forty years ago. While the wine industry continued to boom in the 70's, I was spending free time chasing after the legendary "Volkswagen" (a wild boar in the Frei Brothers Vineyard), or fishing Passalaqua lakes near Healdsburg airport. Those days I was more concerned with over-sized pork chops and trophy bass than what wine would be best for the pairing.

I met up with Paul Bernie at his Dry Creek Valley ranch and vineyard. Paul's a life long Dry Creek farmer and self described "sharecropper." A vineyard manager whose worked the region for decades. Paul tells me, when a vineyard is depleted of nutrients there's few options that can help its demise. Years of farming takes a toll on the land over time.

This is when human influence can best compliment a vineyard through soil enhancement. Many growers "fertigate" to help bring needed nutrients to the vineyards. Fertigation is micro irrigation with water that is fertilized. It's a common practice among many growers.

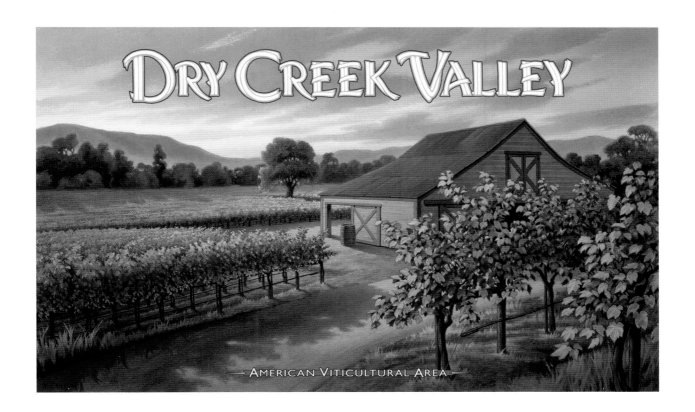

Like in Paul's case, when family takes over the parents' farm, or a farmer's been advised the vineyard land is spent, there is need for soil nourishment. Some owners prefer an organic approach to replenishing depleted nutrients rather than the chemically infused method of fertigation. One sought after method is organic mulching.

This is when they call "the fixer"... Paul Bernie.

So off we went on a hillside roller coaster ride to visit a block of vineyards in Paul's clunky white Toyota truck. He offered to show me some results near Raymond Burrs Vineyards, which were established in the mid 1970's.

The live oak tree branches raking at the window had me bobbing and ducking as we circled the sloping vineyards now rejuvenated by his mulching. Though again, water is an issue here. The table was low. The owner could drill deeper but would tap into Boron, which in heavy concentrations is poison to any vineyard. When I asked Paul how the drought has effected the farmers in the region he simply stated without whining, "Wet or dry... we deal with it."

And just like the farmers deal with the water, they deal with depleting nutrients in the soils. On this particular block, Paul tells me the family had chosen not to take out the existing vineyard. The soil was exhausted but the vines were sentimental-- this agricultural keepsake was once planted and cared for by their grandparents. There are many occasions when another generation cares little for the passing down of things— it's considered "old stuff." No less is there a lack of interest for some in the passing down of fields and those vineyards adorning them. They sell or often rip them out and plant new vines. Not here. This was a family whose thoughts of their mother and father mattered. Their parents had once cared for and worked these vines with the same attention they had cared for in raising them. They felt a kindred spirit to the land. So with the vines ailing, they consulted with the most knowledgable professionals in the field— with hopes of saving them.

And this is Paul Bernie's sweet spot.

Paul's method of organic mulching isn't something new or trendy. He's been taking pumice from local vineyards and oyster grindings from nearby coastal farms for years. He took me to visit his organic lay down yard— a flat vacant lot between Dry Creek Valley vineyards. There was a whale sized pile of crushed oyster composite floundering between vineyards. A "mixologist" himself, Paul was awaiting for the pumice to start coming in so that he could prepare his calcium fortified concoction. "I use 500 tons a year," he says. Then he points to the beast: a tractor with a contraption that looks fitting of a Star Wars movie prop— a mulching auger jutting abruptly at a 90 degree angle from the tractor's rear.

After a moment of contemplating this bone crusher we headed back to Paul's truck. He shows me where his wife plants vegetables each season and sells them to the local markets. As he's pointing to the area I noticed he was wearing sandals. I'd heard from locals

about this guy whose been working vineyards in sandals his entire life— pruning, advising, consulting for RRV grape growers for decades— in sandals. I was intrigued.

We've all heard reference to working individuals as "boots on the ground." Some grape growers today are referring to workers in the vineyards as " boots in the field." So naturally I was intrigued by this bare foot approach. This was "sandals in the vineyards."

The notion reflected a more personal, meaningful approach to working the vines. Certainly the loose soil, dust and moisture influenced a greater touch with the earth. The feel of insect life upon his sun-browned feet and vegetation between his knuckled toes meant a closer association with the land. I wondered if there was a systemic connection, some Biodynamic association or organic meaning behind Paul's barefoot approach. Maybe he was onto something here. So when I asked Paul with great anticipation why this connection with the earth— what was the reason for not wearing boots all these years? He replied quite frankly...

"My feet get hot."

Okay. Well, whoever said "never let the truth get in the way of a good story" hadn't shared it with Paul Bernie. I left my visit here knowing that with Dry Creek Valley farmers there was little embellishing what happens in the field.

Another sub-appellation of the North Coast AVA, just south east of the Russian River Valley, is the Sonoma Valley. It was here at St. Anne's Crossing, formerly the site of

SONOMA VALLEY

— AMERICAN VITICULTURAL AREA —

St. Francis Winery, where I learned the craft of winemaking alongside their first winemaker Bob Roberstson. This was during their boutique days, long before the winery moved down to bigger digs. It was a time when an emerging varietal called Merlot was coming into its own. I was introduced to Andre Tcheldcheff and Bruno Benzinger. My sister met her future husband while working here, and it was Joe Martin, the founder of St.Francis, who graciously provided the winery for their wedding reception. I now have three amazing nephews due to this communion of lives whose ultimate journey began here.

The Sonoma Valley itself is rich with history. Early missionaries like San Francisco Solano planted vineyards here in the 1820's. One of California's first official wineries, Buena Vista, was established here in 1857 and remains an icon today. Further west along Highway 12 is Chateau St. Jean— constructed in the 1920's by a wealthy iron and lumber Michigan couple, it became a founded winery in 1973. Today, Chateau St. Jean's highly scoring Cing Cepage' Cabernet Sauvignon is crafted by acclaimed winemaker Margo Van Staaveren, with 2017 being her 37th harvest here.

From Carneros to Kenwood, the eastern slopes of the Sonoma Valley are draped beautifully in vineyards. Names like Kenwood, Gundlach Bundschu, Kunde, Lasseter, and Gloria Ferrer Caves and Vineyards are among the many fine wineries that can be found here. Established in 1981, this sub-appellation is one of California's most iconic wine regions, producing quality wines from vineyards thriving in its fertile soil. Throughout the Sonoma Valley there are nearly a dozen soil series; the fruit greatly influenced by the distinct character and personality of the land. At the region's southern end is Carneros, where the sedimentary soil is marine based. The mountainous areas and bench lands are mostly volcanic based soils that are well draining— producing exceptional varietals like Cabernet Sauvignon, Carneros Chardonnay, Pinot Noir and Merlot.

The allure of Sonoma Valley is in its simplicity. Its rolling hills. Its shouldered hillsides crawling with oak. Many days and nights I've spent with good friends captivated by a full moon rising— its perfect symmetry slowly launching free of a ridge top; its glowing presence casting shadows in the night. This region has brought well known men and women to romanticize its place in history— none more capturing its abundant beauty than Jack London, a grape grower himself, who wrote of the Valley:

"The grapes on a score of rolling hills are red with autumn flame. Across Sonoma Mountain, wisps of sea fog are stealing. The afternoon sun smolders in the drowsy sky. I have everything to make me glad I am alive. I am filled with dreams and mysteries. I am all sun and air and sparkle. I am vitalized, organic."

For several years I lived in a house that bordered Jack London's State Park in the Sonoma Mountains. It was a small house whose foundation was carved into the steep mountain slope. A large deck overlooked a portion of Glen Ellen and the Sonoma Valley. It was near St. Francis Winery and it was home, where I lived for several years before moving back to Santa Rosa.

Santa Rosa is Sonoma Valleys western neighbor. Its population has exploded over the years while its roads have remained much the same. If you travel north of Santa Rosa on Highway 101 and turn on River Road you can shake the traffic, but not the beauty of the vineyards! It's everywhere until you reach Guerneville. And a dozen miles west of this Bohemian river town you'll be abruptly stopped by cliffs, with barnacled rock formations and the clapping waves of the Pacific Ocean applauding you. For you have arrived.

It is the end of the road here if you're heading west, at least until you hit Hawaii. The Pacific Ocean greets the traveller like no where else on the West Coast. If the fog slicken cattle guards don't stop you, the turnouts will, and for a good cause... the views are immense. The Pacific Coastline's presence not only defines some of the most visually appealing vistas in the state, but defines Fort Ross-Sea View, an AVA federally granted in 2012. Its designation championed in great part by Linda and Lester Schwartz, owners of Fort Ross Vineyards whose estate lays closest to the ocean's steeped, and treacherous beach land.

The region's first wine came from vineyards planted by the Russians who occupied the land here in 1812, whose "lost" Palermo varietal from Peru was said to have been the region's first varietal plantings. Since then, during the 60's and '70's, individuals came to the region as hippies, organic farmers, and gorilla pot farmers. They were back-to-the-earth hipsters, men and women raising communal families, nonconformists moving in among the more conventionally established cattle ranchers.

While the region moved forward a farmer named Michael Bohan decided to plant one acre of Zinfandel. This was in 1972. There were no wine growers here because the "experts" told them grape growing was not possible. It couldn't be done. It's too cold. But for the nonconformist like Bohan, it was more daring to dream what could be, rather than be told what couldn't. So he planted.

> "It was more daring to dream what could be, rather than be told what couldn't."

It was the beginning of something greater than what any grape grower could have hoped for. Bohan's endeavor was a success. This led to more varietal plantings like Pinot Noir and Chardonnay. Eventually, after decades of remote coastal challenges and naysayers, the dreams of a few have become the reality for many. And so, at bluffs above 900 feet, sunlight shines upon these vineyards reaching elevations as high as 2000.

Today, more than a dozen wineries have built foundations upon this dream. There is Nobles Winery to the north, Hirsch in the middle, and Fort Ross and Wild Hog to the south. There is something romantic about these vineyards that covet the land by the sea. There is an allure found here that goes beyond the syrupy love knots occasionally felt in one's gut when experiencing personal attraction. And, as I looked with Lester Schwartz from atop this steepened Fort Ross vineyard, viewing the fog blanketed ocean

FORT ROSS-SEAVIEW

AMERICAN VITICULTURAL AREA

K·ERICKSON

below, the feeling was profound. It was overwhelming– that this stunning presence, embraced by world class wines, was pioneered by one man's vision. Today Lester is living it– a benefactor of Bohan and others who have contributed to the dream.

The region has come far since those "24 planked-dwellings" and garden settlements recorded by the first Russians. It is now a thriving wine appellation encompassing a total of 27,500 acres with presently 520 planted in vineyards. The varietals most prominent in the region are Pinot Noir and Chardonnay, with a host of others including a Cape Town favorite, Pinotage– a cross between Pinot and Cinsault (a Rhône varietal). Introduced in 1925 by Stellenbach University Viticulure professor Abraham Izak Perold, Lester and Linda brought the varietal from South Africa to the region in the 1970's. At the time only 22 acres were known to exist in the country.

Lester reminds me that this land was once occupied by the indigenous Pomo Indians, who thrived here for thousands of years, and referred to their home as, "Top of Land." This reference to place had resonated with the Schwartz's so much that they labelled a Pinot Noir vintage in memory of the indigenous people whose lives once embraced this land– land they now call their own. The Schwartz's also pay homage to American cowboy poet and outlaw Black Bart, who was recorded to have robbed a stagecoach here. The old stagecoach trail remnants are still running through a portion of their property.

We stood at the edge of a vineyard slope embraced by blocks of Pinot Noir and Chardonnay. Behind us the fog was teasing the coastline at its fringes. Lester turned to me, his face was shrouded by his canvas styled hat. He took in a healthy chest of air and with his charmed South African accent asked, "Can you smell it?" A brief moment passed.

"The air is like champagne," he said.

This was no Brian Williams embellishing the truth. Not here. On top of this steep slope embraced by thriving blocks of vineyards, the air is fortified by the ocean's presence. The definable notes of fog, forest, earth and sea filled my preceptors. We indulged in it– the ocean and lands presence. On this remote vineyard mountainside we were drinking from the same vast bucket of blended air the vines were breathing from. And I was feeling the buzz.

I had become awakened. My senses widened. I could see further. I felt invigorated because I was standing at the edge of something far greater than myself. I realized how sobering this place called Fort Ross-Sea View really is, and how profoundly grateful I was to share in the "drinking" of its champagne air.

Upon leaving Fort Ross-Sea View I made my way through the Alexander Valley, and stopped at Jordan Winery whose off-road estate appears to be from another land– like Napa. Further into the valley I dropped in at Young Estate Vineyards whose local history has seen five generations of farmers tending crops.

"There is something romantic about these vineyards that covet the land by the sea."

CALISTOGA

— AMERICAN VITICULTURAL AREA —

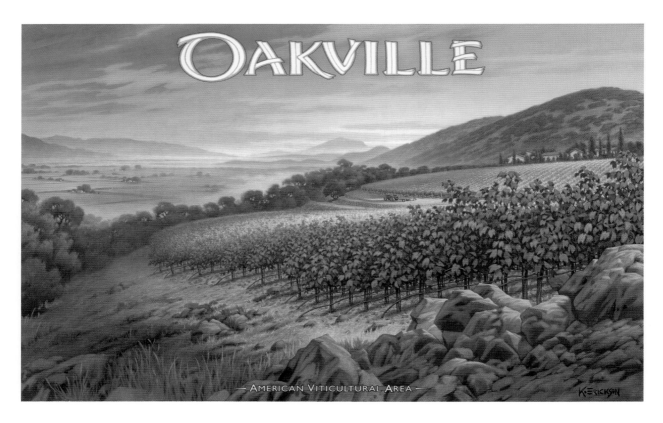

OAKVILLE

— AMERICAN VITICULTURAL AREA —

As the highway moved further along, I passed wineries like Peter Michael and Speedy Creek of Knights Valley. Turning onto Tubbs Lane in Calistoga I visited Chateau Montelena. It didn't disappoint. Its magnificence overwhelms you. I walked into the tasting room; it was swank. The crowd was sophisticated. It felt like I was at a Red Carpet premier for some tent pole movie and the buzz was not merely about the wines or its present harvest but the stuff iconic stories are made of— like the Judgement of Paris.

This historical event was the room's centerpiece. Here copies of the Time's article written by renowned Times columnist George Taber were stacked upon the shelf, and free for the taking. Down the hall a vintage of the original bottle that won the judgment was displayed with ceremonial delight. Copies of accolades by numerous writers regarding the award stuffed the pages of a vinyl folder. The floor director even pointed out the displaying video on the tasting room wall, showing clips of Bottle Shock. And why not? This chosen 1973 Chardonnay is today an object member of the American Dream. The Smithsonian Somms are now serving the infamous bottle up to the masses for the viewing— pairing it with the likes of Armstrong's moon suit, Alexander Bells telephone and the Declaration of Independence. I'd say that's pretty good company. I'd also say if "some of them were my grapes" that helped to influence the wine sitting beside Lincoln's hat, I'd want some of that.

So where was the love? Where was the Bacigalupi or Russian River Association? It was nowhere. It didn't exist. Not in conversation, not in framed reference on the walls, not merely a whisper of the wine's true origin— that being grapes from another appellation. Of course, they were Sonoma County sourced grapes, and this was Napa.

If "sense of place" matters— if terroir is key to the wines journey (which I, and most every wine enthusiast will agree on)— why then are the Bacigalupi grapes or its terroir not mentioned or even referred to as part of the story's historic journey?

I asked a director at Chateau Montelena about this historical void and she reminded me that the present guests had five bottles to taste and the staff move through them "rather quick," so discussing these issues wasn't time effective. Fair enough? I guess. Maybe. The crowd was large. There really wasn't time to get into depth regarding Bacigalupi's association— regarding the varietal of significance, appellation, or the people who planted the grapes that helped bring this wine to greatness.

Yet, if the greatest story ever told about an American wine exempts the seminal elements contributing to its resounding success, and if place matters, then its beginnings must surely have relevance; not as a side kick, but with the same importance that reflects the wines most significant factor... terroir.

Certainly Mike Grgich's craft, his master influence as a winemaker, was paramount to the wine's overwhelming success. It was his wine that stumped the French nonbelievers, leaving them literally blind-sided at their own masked tasting.

So, I had hoped to speak with this iconic winemaker. I heard he was in St. Helena that day, but a hard man to reach and whose health was presently under the weather. At Grgich Hills I spoke with Justin Hills, whose father Austin E. Hills is partners with Grgich. Justin and I spoke at length.

When I asked about the sourcing of grapes that led to the Paris judgement, even Justin stated there were "several growers around the county claiming to have supplied the grapes." I explained to Justin that the Bacigalupi's have a copy of the original weigh tag from Chateau Montelena; that in my interview with Helen, it was Grgich who had called her to announce the wonderful news... that it was her and Charles's grapes that were delivered to Chateau Montelena. I have a photo of George Taber, Mike Grgich, and Charles Bacigalupi together celebrating the news.

There is no debating the fact Chateau Montelena owned the grapes. They weighed them. They paid the grower. Their winemaker crafted the wine beautifully. They bottled the vintage and rightfully claimed the news. There's not much that wasn't theirs, other than from where a portion of the grapes had come from— picked from a block of vineyards off Westside Road in the Russian River Valley.

There is little questioning Napa Valley's stature. Its iconic presence is dizzying. With a handful of distinguished sub-appellations it is the undisputed wine growing champion of the New World— California's vineyard centerpiece. Napa's been drawing talent and affluent

"Its iconic presence is dizzying... It is the undisputed wine growing champion of the New World– California's vineyard centerpiece."

personalities from around the world for years. Its acclaimed AVA draws corporate pairings to the region like that of the Culinary Institute of Art in St Helena, whose past alumni have garnered chefs like Grant Chatz, Roy Choi, Cat Cora, and Anthony Bourdain; in Yountville, the French Laundry restaurant provides world-renowned dinning reflecting the very best in cuisine; and the region attracts acclaimed artists and photographers from around the globe who travel here to study its allure with lens and brush.

Does it make Napa "thou art more holy?" No. It means the region is further ahead of the curve. They've recruited star talent. They've "vineyard the land" to its potential. Their moment of light in this ever changing industry shines brighter upon them, financially able to build castles, create dream lands and dazzling event centers. They also have a powerful advantage with financial backing that many regions don't. This luxury affords cutting edge technology that leads to wine making innovation and increased market savvy. Money matters.

And the money continues pouring into this thirty mile long stretch of revered Napa Valley land. California's first AVA has a Mediterranean climate— something only 2 percent of the world has to offer. Averaging about two miles in width, the Napa Valley bottomland and hillside vineyards grace the region with close to 45,000 planted acres. This may not be huge in numbers, but in the business of fine wine rarely does size matter. Quality is king. It trumps yield. Many of the grape growers reaping rewards with varietals like Cabernet Sauvignon, Pinot Noir, Zinfandel, Merlot, and Chardonnay say they farm to grow less. They boast about it. They are in search of quality, not quantity. They work in many ways to achieve this. Dry farming, sourcing select fruit from neighboring vineyards, reducing bunch per cane through canopy management— all of this to increase the grapes character and flavor intensity.

This is Napa Valley's splendor. Taste. It has defined California as a world leader in the wine industry with a variety of celebrity names that run the course of Silverado Trail. They are the glamor squad. The 15 iconic sub-appellations defining themselves; like Calistoga, St Helena, Oakville, Los Carneros, Rutherford, Stags Leap District, Atlas Peak, Yountville and more. It is where talent thrives. Supporting this region of approximately 500 wineries are the many wine labs, the insectaries, tech advisors and vineyard managers. There are consultants like "the Dirt Doctor," Paul Skinner, who is so high in demand one has a hard time catching up with him. Is it any wonder? I mean, the dirt here along this Silverado Trail is so cherished (think Rutherford Dust) I imagine they beat it out of the rugs, scoop it into jars, and truck it back to the vineyards from where it came.

And it's no wonder. When you figure in the cost of real estate here, there's some serious green invested in this dirt— both in color and money. The Domaine Chandon bubbles rising to the top of these champagne glasses aren't the only rising effervescents, there's a real estate bubble happening.

RUTHERFORD

— AMERICAN VITICULTURAL AREA —

ST. HELENA

AMERICAN VITICULTURAL AREA

The North Bay Business Journal states the cost of a premium Napa agricultural acre in 1950 was approx $1000.00. Presently, the cost of an agricultural acre in Napa runs an average of $300,000– the most expensive in the country. The cost of a Silverado Napa Valley estate? In the millions. The cost of a Napa Valley winery? Priceless. There seems to be no end to the escalating property values. In fact, the North Bay Business Journal states that by 2050 the cost of a premium Napa agricultural acre could fetch a million.

Maybe beating the dirt out of things really isn't that far fetched.

In many ways, to travel the Silverado Trail is to experience a wine coma. Ride the wine train. Treat yourself to a walk among the mansions. Book a multi-million dollar wedding at a wine castle. Tour the newest faux wine chateaus. Soar above the Valley in the comfort of a glider or hot air balloon. The Silverado Trail is branding itself as the Disneyland of Drinkability– a sense of place for all to share, splashed with a pairing of spectacular!

When I left the Silverado Trail it was like stepping off a cruise ship. The fun was over. The wallet was lighter. My liver was weaker and my waistline had become measurably bigger.

It was a hangover based on pure indulgence.

Has this cruise ship feel and theme park adventure distanced the region from the intimacy it once delivered? Maybe. But who cares? Not these guys, and for legitimate reasons. Who needs intimate when grand is more– when grand is nothing short of glorious? And glory sells. While the costs continue to rise in tourist shops, tasting rooms and on store shelves, the region is catapulting itself forward. It is suiting the economic needs of local businesses, and more importantly, its investors.

I don't think quaint is what matters, unless you ask the neighbors who live here. Growth has been an ongoing concern for the people living along the Silverado Trail for years. Its local newspaper, the Napa Valley Register, reports in a 2015 article, "Napa County is convening a summit to gauge if winery growth has become a runaway train." Apparently the locals aren't feeling the agricultural love. A few could give a bung about the bottle. They're looking to put a moratorium on the local wine industry's monumental growth to better their own quality of life. Who can blame them? The traffic's gotten so bad I wouldn't be surprised if they started vetting tourists arriving at the County's border– mostly looking for non imbibers gawking at the region's beauty, threatening to put a cork in the flow of traffic while not spending a nickel on wine.

Yet, with all of its European flare, wonderment, and vacationland appeal, Napa remains one of the most celebrated and affluent wine region's in the world. Its so beloved by the jet-setting crowd one has to wonder... why would anyone want to fly to Europe when France exits here? It is a grape growing island

of its own, a world away.

Will this appellation one day be topped in prominence by another? There are emerging regions circling above the straw bisque summer hills and fettered green valleys garnishing the Napa Valley– regions that may one day draw the same wealth, the same affluence and stature as the glamour squad does along the Silverado Trail.

But for today, it's impossible not to enjoy the ride.

North of Napa is the dry, elevated hills of Lake County. For decades, Lake County has sourced grapes to those talented and financially backed wineries south of them. Today, it is a wine region garnering accolades of its own. What was once a pass through region, has become a new destination.

Unlike years past, much of Lake County grapes no longer have to travel. They can, and are being lovingly crushed at home. For those grapes it means no more bumpy rides over mountain borders; no more bunches squeezed into gondolas or chubby plastic bins; no more long goodbyes through strange valleys to be destined to another region– transported by smoking ten wheelers. Sure, it could be worse. Grapes in the hands of Napa and Sonoma County winemakers with notable talent isn't a bad way to go. Just ask Grgich.

There are still wineries in Napa sourcing Lake County grapes like Fore Family Vineyards, whose Cobb Mountain Vineyard wines are produced and bottled in Napa. For those growers whose grapes remain at home, whose wineries have become financially independent of sources

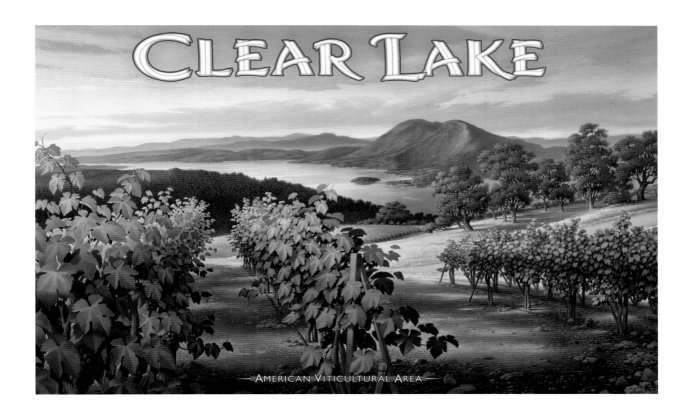

CLEAR LAKE

— AMERICAN VITICULTURAL AREA —

outside the county, it means local growth. By no longer having to cross the county to be branded by another vintner, means a branding of their own. It's become a celebration for not only the growers, but residents who have begun to raise their glasses and cheer this much needed economic influx.

And the party's just started.

Resident grape growers throughout the county are planting with abundance. There are seven sub-appellations included in the county: Red Hills, Kelsey Bench, Big Valley District, Clear Lake, Benmore Valley, Guenoc Valley and High Valley, with varying soils of Franciscan, volcanic and alluvial. In the High Valley, where elevations reach 3,000 feet, the individual grape is protected by a paternal force– that force is the grape's skin. The constant light that bears down at these elevations forces the grape's skin to thicken; much more so than in lower regions, ultimately protecting the procreating part of itself, that being its seed.

Local families who have been growing grapes high and low in Lake County for decades are saying, "I told you so," and new vintners are touting progress and taking the region by storm... literally.

From the Red Hills appellation to the Kelseyville Bench, the volcanic association is shaking this region. Here you'll find labels like *Eruption, Lava Flow, Obsidian Ridge* and *Dynamite*, just to name a few. Though walnut groves, pear orchards and pot farms are among crops grown in the region, it is the vineyard that has taken hold of this unique land where obsidian chunks are as common as volcanic outcroppings.

In 1960, Lake County recorded to have about 100 acres of planted grapes; today there are close to 10,000. Wineries are rising out of the volcanic ashen soils to establish themselves. Tasting rooms are bringing fresh life and unprecedented cheer.

It means more family at the table. It becomes a community connection not only for the grape growers, but for the restaurants, cafes, and tourist shops. It is the revival of a waning economic region. Speak to most locals and they'll say "thank goodness for the grapes."

Here in Lake County there is a colossal force of nature that rears its ugly head when the season of green hills turn brown. It is one that threatens vineyards– the region's wild land fires. Though vineyards may serve as fire breaks, a land fire storm is relentless. Its fury can devastate everything in its path, smothering vineyards, scorching vines at its fringes, and tainting grapes. Due to the seasonal association with wild fires in the area, grape growers have legitimate concerns. Harvest is likely happening. When grape skins absorb undesirable levels of the lingering smoke, damage can occur. It can leave the grapes' finished flavor crawling with notes that have been horrifically described as "a wet ash tray." Not only making the wines unpalatable, but an entire vintage met with ruin. Fortunately during the usual peak of fire season the red varietals have undergone veraison and are less susceptible to "smoke taint."

On a hot afternoon in Kelseville at the Studebaker Cafe, I sat with Debra Sommerfeld, president of the Lake County Wine Growers Association. The air was hazy outside. Two terrifying fires had recently spared Lake County vineyards– they were the Jerusalem and Rocky fires. Debra indicated the PPM (parts per million) of smoke was not an issue. She was assured by local growers that the grapes were in fine shape. Easterly winds had carried the smoke swiftly away– the winds that caused these same fires to fuel had been a Godsend.

Then, weeks later it hit.

There was no containing what would become one of the region's worst wild land fire in history. The Valley Fire. More than 35 wineries and close to 10,000 acres of vineyards were threatened throughout the region. Langtry Estate Vineyards was spared, but the fire consumed an out building– stopping at the borders of its 23,000 acre estate. Shed Horn Cellars was leveled. Growers couldn't gain access to their vineyards due to road closures. The firestorm travelled 40,000 acres overnight. Its monstrous and random activity was so unchartered, Cal Fire models couldn't predict them. It was the firestorm from hell burning vineyards, choking vines and tainting grapes.

The Valley fire took approximately 1,000 homes and consumed several towns in less than a day. It leveled portions of Middletown, burnt through Cobb along the 175, and threatened Kelyseville. The historic Hoberg House I had passed weeks earlier on my travels to the region was burned to the ground. What seasoned firefighters

MENDOCINO

— AMERICAN VITICULTURAL AREA —

K ERICKSON

had deemed "long over due" had suddenly happened, turning wine country landscape a dozen shades of grey.

Beyond the flames, north of Lake County, is another viticulture area establishing itself as a significant player in the wine industry... Mendocino County. This mountainous region, covering over 2,000,000 acres includes ten American Viticultural areas with more under consideration.

Scattered in small lots are 18,000 acres of planted vineyards, 20 percent of which is certified organically grown— the largest organic percentage in the state. This includes a large percent of Biodynamic acreage amounting to nearly 700 acres. The region is so lovingly stigmatized by organic that those outside the county who chirp organic, look organic, or grow organic are referred to as being "So Mendocino." The county brands itself as "Americas greenest wine region."

It's also one of America's greenest outdoor pot growing regions, including itself in the notorious "Emerald Triangle." While the grape harvest is underway, "Trimmers" from all over the country come to Mendocino to harvest and crop the sticky buds. They have for decades. Bud shapers like winemakers, know their craft.

Grape growing in Mendocino is dependent on smaller blocks of vineyards due to the rugged forest landscape. A typical vineyard averages 10 to 14 acres. The region's best known varietals are

Pinot Noir, followed by Cabernet Sauvignon, Zinfandel, and Merlot. And as the region grows so has the variety of grapes planted, like Alsace varietals Gewurtztraminer, Pinot Gris and Riesling.

Among the ten AVA's in Mendocino County, Anderson Valley is the most acclaimed with its Pinot Noir rocking the region's string of hits– Goldeneye Winery in Philo provided their Pinot Noir for the 2012 Obama inauguration.

Whether you score a tasting trip among oak groves, find yourself perched on mountain tops or lounging in a tasting room shaded by magnificent Coastal Redwoods, each of Mendocino's sub-appellations reflects a foggy, cool terroir uniquely its own.

Today, hundreds of wineries throughout the entire North Coast offer exquisite tasting rooms splashed with style and body. They are as diverse as the region's own varietals. Whether intimate, rustic, modern, or funky in ambience, they offer the wine enthusiast a tasting experience found no where else in the country. They provide space to relax indoor and out. From the elevated foothills of Lake County, to the Sonoma and Napa Valley, along the Fort Ross-Seaview AVA, and north to Mendocino, the tasting rooms offer spectacular vistas and iconic settings, contributing to the immense success the North Coast wine industry experiences today.

For wine enthusiasts the tasting room defines a spirit of relaxation. Its communion is not simply with the indigenous environment. They are "buzzkill" free zones. They take us away from the politics and social media drama– from the "Debbie Downer" stories that suck the fresh air from us, and the ugly news stories that rock our world.

Not in the tasting room. Here they pour, pare, charm and comfort. They are ambassadors of good times, hosting, and sharing in California's North Coast abundance. Like the best of hotels the wineries have hospitality directors to insure a visit is one to be remembered. Few industries deliver the care and unequivocal attention to a place of welcome. To taste the estate wines is to share the same sunshine, fog and rainy days the local vineyards embrace. It is a place where one becomes more than members of a "club" or mere visitors within its walls– but a place wine enthusiasts discover moments of local distinction. Whether it's the terroir or the winemaker's craft the character found in the glass is distinctly its own.

Personally, there have been no tasting room visits more profound than my morning visit with Helen Bacigalupi. The room was quaint and surrounded by oaks and subtle hills. The estate vineyards nearby had been cared for by Charles and Helen Bacigalupi for decades. We talked at length about the history of the winery and the region, and when our conversation led to its challenges regarding the drought, Helen scuffed. Like most who've seen droughts come and go, Helen is a farmer in touch with place. The sunny mornings, the ebbing fog lying low over the valley has for nearly a century defined home for her. She pointed to a slideshow of historic photos on the tasting room flat screen– a black and white image of the Russian River flooding the lower vineyard faded in.

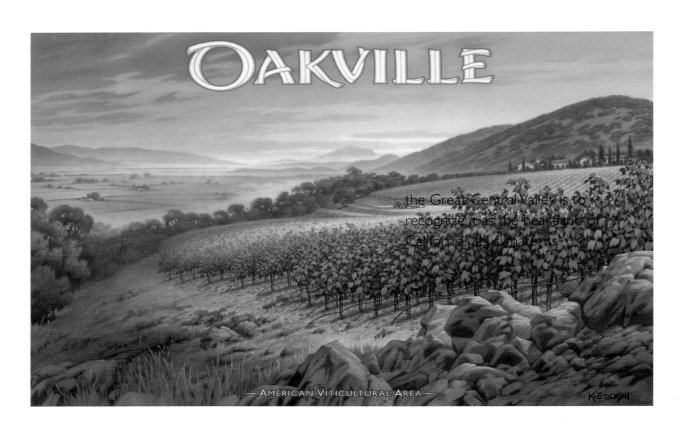

OAKVILLE

the Great Central Valley is to
recognize it as the heartland of
California., its climate its

— AMERICAN VITICULTURAL AREA —

NAPA VALLEY

— AMERICAN VITICULTURAL AREA —

46

Helen turned to me and nodded with optimistic certainty, "It will come again" she said, referring to the states lack of water. Helen's words resonated with the voice of age– with wisdom that comes from life experiences. She then smiled reverently as an image of her late husband Charles appeared. Together they had succeeded in fulfilling a dream passed onto their grandchildren Nicole and Katherine.

As the slide show images continued, a seemingly unremarkable block of vineyards appeared. It was the vineyard that produced the grapes bought by Chateau Montelena that contributed to the iconic wine Grigich so masterfully crafted. In my North Coast travels little was mentioned of their Russian River Valley vineyard. The French judges' scores have been touted. Chateau Montelena's branding of the event has been marketed. Grigich has been inducted into the Wine Hall of Fame. Hollywood's promoted the movie. Times writer George Taber gained notoriety breaking the story. What has been spoken of the wine's beginning has, at best, been only grape whisperings. Yet we know a percentage of the infamous grapes that contributed to this seminal event were sourced from the Russian River Valley appellation– a place where barns are more prominent than castles and a seemingly unremarkable vineyard ultimately helped bring spectacular to a Napa County bottle. A vintage 1973 Chardonnay so esteemed it sits in the Smithsonian today, crowning itself as the wine industry's most celebrated moment in the New World.

THE CENTRAL VALLEY

It was an early afternoon in June that I had the pleasure of speaking with winemaker Michael Blaylock in his office at Quady Winery. When I asked Michael what his thoughts were regarding a "sense of place" here in the Central Valley, he looked at me for a moment, and then with his infectious laugh turned the question on me...

"And what sense do YOU make of this place?" he asked.

I wasn't ready for that one. This guy's good. He's also approachable and one of those guys you feel like you've known all your life. But, he had me.

We both glanced out the window towards the neighboring vineyards, and as if something else caught our attention we continued discussing the region's past history and present challenges. The question of "sense of place" was for the moment unanswered.

And maybe for good reason.

You see, the Central Valley grape growing region is in itself a quandary. By that, I mean it's neither an AVA nor a single region, but actually two distinct regions— two separate valleys coming together as one, whose main bodies and associated rivers meet and flow into the Sacramento-San Joaquin River Delta.

With two of the most prolific producing appellations in the state located here, the Madera AVA and the Lodi AVA, it is considered the heartland of America's colossal wine growing region. Fanning the rural landscape across more than a dozen counties are 17 American Viticultural Areas. The land speaks of the region's suitability and of the grape growers immense success with varietals including Chardonnay, French Colombard, Chenin Blanc, Zinfandel, Cabernet Sauvignon, and Muscat.

And if you think that was a mouthful, consider this: eons ago this entire area was an expansive sea with massive fault upliftings and steeped valleys that evolved into fertile marshlands where prehistoric life foraged and strolled. Over millions of years, the decaying Pacific and Eastern mountains filled the valley with deposits, lifting the region to its present elevation of an average 200 feet.

MADERA

MADERA
WINE TRAIL
Welcome

K. ERICKSON

— AMERICAN VITICULTURAL AREA —

Along with wine grapes, thriving in this fertile soil are over 230 different crops– more than any other region in the nation. The Great Central Valley is the undisputed center of California agriculture; it is the hand that feeds the world.

Farmers have been harvesting grapes here for decades. In the mid 1800's, Jonathan Holt Dodge built a large estate in Stockton, where the Holt house still stands today as Sorelle Winery. In the 1860's, the Hoffman family homesteaded 400 acres in Lodi that is now home to Heritage Oak Winery. In 1906, Franzia bought Ripon Ranch, and after prohibition came Gallo– both growing to become juggernauts within the wine industry. Among these pioneers were also hard working laborers, water architects, and engineers whose past efforts brought sustenance to the region.

But my thoughts of traveling to this "great" Valley so drenched with history were filled with skepticism– mostly due to highway 99. It was always that long boring drive to see family, and the long return back home. I just wasn't feeling it. It's not like it's a hard drive from Southern California. Just follow the attractive, highly poisonous, white and pink oleanders north– past the dairy farms, pot bellied silos, tractor stores, pallet bone yards, industrial junkyards and stores advertising themselves Texas style, like *Boot Barn*.

It wasn't until I took the exit and left the ninety mile-per-hour crowd to fight amongst themselves, did things quiet. Life slowed. Here, the crunch of commercial and industry leftovers faded, while the land softened and came to life with flat stretches of cultivated bliss. This is Vineyard Country– city sized

blocks of vineyards encompassing thousands of acres; defined by sweet varietals like Orange and Black Muscat, Port varietals like Tinta Madeira, and those table grapes we so love to snack on... Thompson seedless.

The open land welcomes you with smiling vinyards at every turn. Its approachable. Its presence shouting its grand hellos. This makes for the beauty of leaving the beaten pavement. In a few minutes the traffic noise disappears and one is embraced by the soothing harmony of vineyards. Lots of them– to the tune of 71 percent of wine grapes grown in the state.

In the northern part of the Central Valley, the Sacramento-Delta region, are wineries like Bogle Vineyards, Gnarly Head, and Abundance Vineyards. To the south you'll find Birdstone Winery, Fasi Estate and renowned port makers like Quady Winery. Bordering Quady is the eight hundred pound gorilla in the room... Constellation Wine Group's Mission Bell Winery.

In the out-lying regions, set among the foothills near Madera, are many smaller wineries like Westbrook Wine Farms. These wineries bunch like Muscat clusters– delightfully crowding the countryside– but none so defines "port" authority like Ficklin Vineyards. The Ficklin family roots go back to the purchase of the land in 1918 by Walter Ficklin and his wife Mame. Their farming began with fruit and raisins; it wasnt until 1946 that the family began their port endeavors in the Portuguese tradition.

I had the pleasure of spending time with Peter Ficklin and his fiancé Denise at the

Ficklin Winery. Here, I discovered what lies at the heart of the Ficklin vineyard— a continuum of place and people. Just as vines grow and grapes mature, so do the best of wineries and those who run them. There's no substituting experience. No embellishing the significance of family history. Not with the Ficklins. Age resonates throughout the winery, where the value of family is synonymous with wine. Ficklin ports are arguably the best in the state if not the country.

Embodied in the winery's Old World cellar is a living, breathing life that cheerfully haunted me the moment I stepped in. Built in the mid 1940's by Walter Ficklin and his sons— Walter Jr. and David— there is no embellishing its place as a historic, living landmark. To understand this best, one needs only to look upon the Adobe brick walls that are constructed from the very soil the cellar stands upon. It is the same earth that sustains its vineyards, that houses the barrels and ages the port.

This iconic work resonates with California's past. Even the arms of the decade old ivy gripping the exterior walls beg to call the cellar its own. The ivy vines climb and cling— they find nourishment from these earthen bricks. Their trunks are old growth themselves.

Inside, I felt a pulse that resonated with some- thing more, something grand and timeless. In this dark, dank environment where cement floors are patinated fittingly with the scent

of Portuguese varietals, is where human influence begins the journey of fortifying and finessing the Tinta Madeira port. Here the wine is put to rest in barrels and grand oak pipes, characterized by their quarter sawn faces, oval stature, and hammered looking bands. I know if I was born a port, this is where I'd want to spend my time chilling out— aging with my best friends and family by my side— growing old with the best of care. Eventually to be liberated from this womb of darkness; my life celebrated and appreciated by others at another time, in another place.

The cellar stands beside the Ficklin's 35 acres of Tinta Portuguese vineyards. It is a living, breathing "place"— a natural symphony inside and out. No one so personifies the selfless nature of the winery's presence than Peter Ficklin, whose family story is as rich in history as its Tawny port is smooth.

Ficklin ports are members of the elite Solera Process (aging wine by fractional blending)— living wines that come from the very first Ficklin barreling. Each bottle contains history of the daunting challenges these fortified wines faced during prohibition. Public outcry and regulations enforced by the Bureau of Prohibition were arduous. The original government lock still dangles from the door where the brandy was stored. The very wood tank where the "Gauger" looked over the shoulder of Ficklin still stands as a testament to the Ficklin's fortitude. The old hand press on wheels is still in use and the old block and tackle still hangs perfectly from the cellar wall. To hear Peter reflect on these artifacts is to understand his reverence for family. It is a reminder of history and of place– a window into the Ficklin family past sustained by the use of primitive tools. Evolving over decades is this continuum of family, whose ties to the land continue to bring warmth, joy, and laughter to the table.

Closer to the town of Madera, among the vast blocks of table grape vineyards, is Quady winery– one of the larger producing wineries along the Madera Wine Trail. The long journey Andrew and Laurel Quady have ventured on is an endeavor defined by deliciousness– seeking excellence in their desert wines, aperitifs and specialty drinks you'll find no where else in the region or throughout the state.

If a winery's story was defined by genre, Quady's would be a romance– a syrupy love tale of passion and seduction. It is the story of a Muscat who has come of age by venturing further into the world– to a mature place where the self proclaimed elite may view her as provocative, flirtatious and sweet beyond measure. But to know her is to understand that she is refined, confidant, and respected by everyone who shares in her company. With names like Electra, Deviation, a Essensia and Vya, she reflects a taste more glamorous and fitting of a model runway than a 750 or 375 ml bottle. And of course she brings with her a host of luxurious companions to the table– fruits, cheeses and decadent chocolates.

Andrew and Laurel Quady have certainly brought desert wines to life, but it is winemaker Michael Blaylock who has, on his own terms, perfected the art of sweet. This perfection is bringing in new crowds. Millennials are educating themselves with wines like the black and orange Muscat, and mixologists are introducing their own cocktails– bringing light to these wines that so elegantly enhance their artful spirits.

Fortunately, I had the chance to sit down with Michael Blaylock in his office to talk about the region and its future. But first, I had a gripe... not with the wines of course, but with the roads. More specifically, with Madera county's forefathers who were either math majors or design engineers because there's an impersonal numbers based road system designed to make travel, well, easy?

I just wasn't feeling it. Sure, cities have their first, second, fourth and those numbered streets in every town– it's common. But Avenue 24 1/2 and 17 3/4 and other impersonal names? You're talking about fractions. This is the agriculture capital of the world. "Why?" I asked Michael. "Why make it so difficult?" He explained to me, laughing at my ignorance, "No, it's the easiest system in the world." He went on to make good sense of why the numbers are where they are on the map. It was simple. Grade school stuff. You add this, add that, and you're over here.

Listen, I hate math. Even simple additions bother me. And when I'm driving Central Valley roads embraced by darling vineyards, I'm looking to relax and view the varietal countryside– not factor in some number to get me there.

As we sat in his office the subject turned from simple math to a Jurassic Park sized issue—something far more complex and colossal... water. That's right, the record drought the state is facing is wreaking havoc, and this Tyrannosaurs Rex has reared its fat neck to bully the lives of many in the Central Valley region. When I asked Michael what his thoughts were regarding this formidable monster, in walks the water champion of the Valley and 4th generation almond grower—Denis Prosperi.

"Here's your man," Michael says with his infectious laugh. It was impossible timing. This was Denis Prosperi... not only the head nut guru of the valley— almond grower extraordinaire— but the most respected vocal Central Valley water authority in the state. A farmer whose passion for growing crops is as important as is his commitment to the valley and those who make a living here. His obvious frustrations with self interest groups and political ignorance regarding water issues today reminded me immediately of that Forrest Gump euphemism, "Stupid is what stupid does."

But Denis doesn't rant. He isn't a bellyacher or subscribe to "poor me's" even as water issues threaten his livelihood. What is threaded in the jeans of this hard working farmer is grit. Like most farmers he's a fixer— a no nonsense, hear me out, common sense man; a fit fireball of a farmer, jacked in wrangler jeans, flannel shirt and ball cap. No doubt the smartest man in the room. Just ask Enron whose attempts to maintain a "Water bank" (turning water into a traded commodity), would have been disastrous to the region if not for men like Prosperi championing the Central Valley's cause.

The over drafting of water here is not only caused by drought, but compounded by shutting off water to the valley's farmers. This forces new wells to be drilled and existing wells to be made deeper, ultimately dropping the water table below historic levels. Water that was once transported to irrigate the fields, is now forced by regulation to flow unobstructed and empty into the ocean. That's right... empty. In 2008, federal regulators put these restrictions in place to largely protect the two inch Delta Smelt from the hazards of "menacing pumps." But this fish population is still declining. And like every great fish story, this one continues to grow. In a report published by the state of California, the federal governments survey trawls— those that count smelt numbers kill more of these endangered fish than the delta pumps do themselves.

It appears these government regulations are based upon "sloppy science" and fish stories gone bad. Here in the Central Valley water is a commodity fueling war; it is the region's life blood. Along highway 99 are billboards that read, "Where water flows, farmers grow." Without the engineered canals and aquaducts delivering this shimmering commodity to these planted acres, agriculture would cease to exist.

And those are fighting words.

But Denis's visit to the winemaker's office wasn't about water, almonds, or even nimrods; he was concerned with the Muscat Canelli clusters on the vines. They were too tight. It was too soon. So Michael excused himself, and he and Denis covered some relevant figures regarding the grapes massing.

"Caneli grape clusters grow tight." Michael explained. As they mature they force themselves upon one another, crowding the bunch. The pressure crushes their thin skins, causing them to weep. This can lead to mold and other issues. Michael fittingly refers to these tight growing Canneli bunches as "hang grenades."

At the end of their conversation they were at an agreement— they were to pick early. And with that, Denis departed. I felt fortunate to have met this vocal California champion and common sense farmer. Though my visit here was short, I learned a great deal about how this place and the people who care for it, resonates with what is best in the winemaker and farmer: honesty, commitment and genuine appreciation of the land.

Upon leaving Quady, I passed the nearby Mission Bell Winery, whose roots were built upon the Italian Swiss Agricultural Colony— now owned by global beverage consumer Constellation. Constellation has its own bottle factory on site. And if you're wondering how many gallons of water it takes to make one glass bottle, versus one almond, I didn't go there. I did leave the great Mission Bell arch to visit smaller wineries that stretch easterly towards the foothills and have established themselves at higher elevations— wineries like Fasi and its neighbor WestBrook Wine Farms, which I had the pleasure of visitng.

Unlike the goliath Mission Bell conglomerate, with its grand arched entrance and sweeping acreage, when I visited Westbrook Wine Farms I had to ask myself, is it really a winery if there is no grand entry— if there is no sign out front stating its very existence? Is it a winery if the road that leads you in cannot accommodate buses, wedding events, or for that matter, tasting strays from Madera's signature wine trail without an invite? Maybe not. Unless the wine made from this hidden, out of the way, quaint cellar is built largely upon one man's vision... a man whose accomplishments are rarely achieved in a lifetime, and whose attention to every detail applies to all aspects of the growing and making of something exceptional.

"...whose attention to every detail applies to all aspects of the growing and making of something exceptional."

Meet Ray Krauss— winemaker, owner, rancher, vineyard manager— and his wife Tammy. They're no strangers to wine, farming and those involved with the Central Valley industry. Ray has worked with Hall of Wine Fame Andre Tcheldcheff. He has also traveled and tasted with wine icon and grocer Darrel Corti, whose involvement within the industry goes back decades.

Their unassuming cellar, with its impressive WWF pulls on the colossal door, tells a story in itself. It's in the details. The winery cellar, hammered and anchored into the granite mountainside, delivers a pleasant ambiance with its solar powered spring water fountain, and the scent of fine wines and oak barrels. The Krauss's do not open their doors to the wine crowd drop-ins. This may be a buzz kill for the day trippers who haven't called ahead for a tasting, but the Krauss's do arrange and welcome scheduled tastings.

Due to its precise spot centered on the California map, Westbrook Wine Farm may be called "California Central." Its elevation is apporxiamtely1500 feet, and in Central Valley terms, that's high– not nose bleed high, but above the fog with an occasional dusting of snow each year. The morning breeze rises gently through the Fait and Accompli vineyard blocks. The air lifting and turning the cordoned and trellised canopies, whips the vines free of dust and dew, lessening the threat of mold. During the evening winds draft down from the mountains and cool the vines. Ray says, "I don't check for sugar." He presses the grapes between his fingers looking for color in the seed. Sugar speaks only for the grape, not the stem. "You can have 30 brix with the stems still green, and if you pick green stemmed fruit, you'll have a green influenced juice."

Ray and Tammy are attentive to their environment and may have gone organic, but the existing cedar treated rails within their property would not qualify for organic certification. They're okay with it. They farm sustainably without certification. They use no pesticides on their 3.5 acres of estate Bordeaux.

Ray first moved into an existing, dilapidated green shack on the property. Not until he had worked the land, planted the vineyard, and ensured the young vines were comfortably taken care of by spring fed irrigation lines, did Ray seek comfort for himself. He then built a house among the oaks, where he and his wife Tammy could overlook the vines.

Ray is the evolving farmer. His lifestyle reflects the independent grape grower who's taken the knowledge of wines to a higher place. Among my time spent traveling, the independent farmer is in far greater touch with place than the public conglomerates whose constant push for profits drives decision making– those with an eye more in touch with ticker tape than bud break. The grape grower is not a thousand miles away from the vineyard environment, conveniently safe in his city bungalow, in a state of the art concrete formed high rise where doors open for him and taxis sweep him off to cocktail parties. There's certainly nothing wrong with this lifestyle. We're all fans of luxury. I know I am. The fair question is– does this personal disconnect from the vineyard make for lesser wine? Maybe not. Gobs of money can help make quality. And having qualified people in place to manage things often amounts to success. Yet, the responsible farmer who works the land and lives upon the same soil– the very earth that runs through his fingers– is in far greater touch with the vineyards. And people in touch with place matter. The rain that falls upon the vineyard, falls upon them. The light that nurtures the grape, warms them. Every element that influences vine growth and grape maturation, that so richly characterizes the wine, flows through the veins of the farmer.

Few public companies share the family connection that farmers like Ray and Tammy do. This lifestyle doesn't make them better winemakers. It doesn't make them martyrs of simplicity. It simply reflects an honest, tangible, living character embodied in the wine. And therein lies a beautiful truth– one so often overlooked... the independent farmer wouldn't change these sacrifices for any city luxury or roof top view. They wouldn't trade their muddy boots for Jimmy Choo shoes, trade their jeans for Armani Suits, or for that matter, trade the dirt, the challenges and their connection to the land for the most citified convenient lifestyle. This dedication to vineyard life is a deeply personal investment. Unlike a public stock offering whose ticker price is paramount to its investors, the farmers investment is simply living by their crops. There is a marriage. It comes first. I have seen it in my travels. Their lives and association with wine speaks not of buttery, jammy, toasted notes so chirped about in the best of wines, but of delicious unspoken notes of the grape growers born by living beside them. That Kodak jingle, "We don't sell cameras we sell memories," applies to the essence of wines themselves. At the heart of every drink there is a moment that is shared by others. And the memories we glean from the drink is immeasurable. Do you think if wines were any less flavored, wine "connoisseurs" would quit drinking them? No. Wines are far greater than the complexities and flavors attributed to them. Certainly we revel in their complexities; we fall over ourselves by their character and delicious distinctions, but the independent grape grower and winemaker define these finer complexities and more. Their communion with place and attention to the vines are the unspoken notes left behind.

Further north, about 100 miles east of San Francisco and closest to the Sacramento-Delta is the Lodi AVA with approximately 90,000 planted acres. Climate, soil and geography here is far diverse from its southern valley neighbors. The region is cooled by Delta breezes which contributes to some tasty, hearty reds— including its flagship Zin.

Transforming the dynamics of the Lodi region is the Trinchero Family Estate's massive production facility. Unlike many of the smaller wineries throughout the region, its footprint is changing the landscape and is a testament to how serious Lodi has become as a major player with prominence in the space.

Extending north of Lodi are AVA's such as the Consumnes, Mokulumne and Sloughhouse. They too are gaining notoriety and making leaps and bounds towards finer wine quality. Zinfandel, Chardonnay, Cabernet Sauvignon, and Sauvignon Blanc are bringing prominence to this northern Central Valley region where the native oak trees define the countryside. To speak of this wine region without its association to the native oak would be like visiting California and not feeling the embrace of its iconic sun. In fact, wineries are naming themselves after their valley favorites. You have wineries like Oak Farm Vineyards, Heritage Oak Winery, Housley's Century Oak, and Oak Ridge all wanting to be associated to this California icon— branding themselves by name and label to these trees so prominent in the Sacramento-Delta region.

Not only are the oaks hugely prevalent in the region, but they represent a relevance that reflects character, balance, and strength— elements all critical to the best wine. The oak is an absolute part of California's Eco system. What the oak takes from vineyard space, it gives back to in its company. The oak enhances soil nutrients and is home to healthy insects. Predator birds, like the Cooper's hawk and red-tailed hawk, perch on its impending limbs— true hunters of native rodents. For centuries the oak has afforded the region's Native American Indians, like the Miwok and

LODI

—AMERICAN VITICULTURAL AREA—

Yokut, sustenance with its abundant yields of acorns. And it once provided shade for the lounging grizzly.

The oaks that have aged for centuries stand as sentinels today through much of the Central Valley– reflecting the farmers toil, the vineyards sustenance, and communion with earth. There are many associations with the oak, it has even found its way into the wines themselves. The use of coopered oak barrels adding natural tannins that soften and curl flavor– adding complexities to the wines. The tree lends itself as furniture to the table, bringing us closer to friends and family where we gather to tell stories, share dreams and create memories that last for a lifetime.

On a Wizard of Oz-like stormy afternoon, when I travelled through miles of vineyards to visit the Heritage Oak Winery, the air was choked with dirt and the vineyards shivered violently– their long canes contorting and leaning eerily sideways. The only thing missing was that creepy jingle and a witchy, bike riding lady dressed in black with a scruffy dog in her basket. It was that scary. The winds dusting the entire region were so fierce they made headlines in the local paper the following day. I half expected to see Dorothy on the front cover clutching Toto in her arms.

It was a great windstorm and a memorable moment for me as I was greeted by an ancient blue oak that stands in the center of the Heritage Oak winery's entrance. It laughed at the prevailing windstorm. I felt calmed by its presence. And as I stood beneath it, the ferocious winds seemed to be nothing more than a hair scrubbing of its upper tangles. While I struggled to stand still beneath it, the Blue Oak stood stoic– cleansing in this remarkable bath. It virtually howled with laughter. It spoke of fortitude and sustainability.

"While I struggled to stand still beneath it, the Blue Oak stood stoic– cleansing in this remarkable bath."

Is it any wonder the owners of Heritage Oak, Tom and Carmela Hoffman, embrace it?

Like the oak, there is a great sense of heritage here. Tom's ties to five generations goes back when the land was homesteaded in the mid eighteen hundreds. They've come a long way. The Hoffman's began their vineyard plantings around the early 1960's with the more popular Tokay table grape. As Tom says, "The more they planted of the table grape, the greater the glut." This lead to less price per ton and growers were forced to plant other table grapes that had not glutted the marketplace. It was during the early eighties that wine grapes staged a renaissance.

Today, Heritage Oak is thriving. The farming practices that the Hoffman's have in place reflect everything that is sustainable without certification. To them, responsible farming is merely common sense. It's an obvious responsibility. The environmental and economic impact they have on the land and community is paramount.

In many ways, generational farmers are tired of being told what to do. They are an independent bunch who are constantly having to deal with issues forced on them like emissions, additives, and water usage. Regulation has become an open spigot of government restrictions, drowning practical farming with bureaucratic fluff. Certainly some regulations are justifiable and necessary but less government intervention is better. Today there's even talk about the Sand Hill

Crane needing take-off room for flight– with all the vineyard land that may be a problem. Will a regulation now be put in place forcing growers to widen vineyard rows for the lanky crane to better lumber and take flight?

It is the younger farmer who generally tends to be more openly acceptable and compliant. The millennium generation has been conditioned to be accommodating to government intervention and grown accustomed to regulation. They've been schooled in the facts and laws that direct them to sign here and dot there.

The old school farmer is more of an independent lot, whose deals were born with a handshake. They've worked the land far longer than many. They've seen what works and what doesn't. They've learned from their mistakes. These farmers are in many ways like the couple who's lived together for years and never married; who don't need a certificate to prove their love for one another. They've nurtured their relationship with the land for decades, and it's working. They are there for each other and those around them. It's understood. To be there for the one you've invested in is more than common sense, it's a commitment to be there for one another for a lifetime. This is the responsible farmer, the grape grower. They will die beside the land before letting it go fallow or allow the community they live among to suffer– this without certification.

Tom, who practices sustainability, is aware of these things critical to the environment. He says, "We don't need a little mark on our label to show we're certified. It doesn't sell wine." He goes on to say, when a tasting

crowd comes through, "They don't look for a yellow mark. They're looking for good wine." This coming from a 5th generation farmer whose land in the Lodi region has been cultivating grapes since the mid 1960's; producing exceptional wines with longevity in mind. It's a sensible practice without the sustainable certificate to frame upon the wall.

Yet Tom's son, who once worked for Lodi's certification program, is a firm believer in SIP certification and believes his father should be a member of Lodi's SIP program.

Tom says respectfully and with a smile, "He and I disagree."

And disagreements will continue to challenge the Central Valley wine industry's future– both north and south. It's the nature of business. This vast stretch of wine country, whose jug wines juiced the vats and filled the pocket books of larger wineries for decades, have found their way. The money is staying at home, leading to wineries producing finer wines of recognition. The region has evolved and is no longer stigmatized by its former bulk wine image.

Leaving the Central Valley was to understand time does not stand still. Not for the farmer, not for the vineyard, and clearly, not for its wines. What lies ahead for the Valley will be defined by future generations whose continued planting and harvesting will not only benefit the grape growers, but the community, the state and world hunger itself.

All it needs is water to survive.

There is an incredible legacy here that speaks

of past generations who have made a tangible, organic breathing life from a vacant, parched and fallow land. The canals, levees, and aqueducts drawing from the rivers are its lifeblood. Take the water and you take the farm, the food, and the wine; the heartland regresses, returning to its former self, becoming dry, distant, and fallow. The architects and engineers of the Central Valley's vast water system, and the farmers and laborers are responsible for bringing life to the land here. They are the true champions feeding the nation— providing food and drink to the masses. They have cared for the valley for decades, many going back generations. They have saved it from drought, disease, pestilence and flooding. And those who believe in the saying, "They cannot save it from fools," have not met Denis Prosperi. Agricultural life will be sustained because of them.

As I traveled further south along the "Oleander Highway," where earlier in my travels that boring sameness seemed to drag on for days, the time passed as fleeting as the vineyards. The void of monotony was filled with a sense of wonder. The thought of what I was leaving behind was no longer a quandary. The region speaks of change and abundance. I thought of the mystery of this Great Valley— the promise and the fortitude of those men and women working the land here. A vast land, still intimately defined by the farmer. It led me to the late morning visit I had with winemaker Michael Blaylock and the question I had asked him that he so fittingly turned on me...

"And what sense do you make of this place?"

A lot I was now certain of... to make sense of

the Great Central Valley is to recognize it as the heartland of California. Its climate, soils and iconic sun are unique to all the world— where vineyards thrive and agriculture grows in abundance. It is a land defined by the joining of two great valleys— sustained by the best of two main rivers that come together as one.

And here I was in the heart of it, driving the long road home.

THE CENTRAL COAST
American Viticultural Area

When Rusack's Cessna Carravan touched down at Santa Ynez airport there was cause to celebrate... another Santa Catalina Island harvest had successfully been delivered. After having crossed over 22 miles of the Pacific Ocean, the grapes would now be offloaded and trucked to Rusack's Ballard Canyon Winery, where under the guidance of winemaker Steven Gerbac, the vintage would be produced and bottled in the Central Coast— the largest AVA in the state.

From Santa Barbara County to San Francisco Bay, the Central Coast AVA stretches along 250 miles of California coastline. There are approximately 100,000 acres of planted grapes throughout five counties: Santa Clara, Contra Costa, Monterey, Santa Barbara and San Luis Obispo. The region's maritime breezes and soil enriched by former sea bed floors has made for the perfect pairing— the terroir is influencing a diversity of varietals and producing world class wines.

Spanning the entire Central Coast are renowned sub-appellations like Arroyo Grande Valley, Paso Robles, Santa Clara Valley, Santa Lucia Highlands, Sta. Rita Hills, Happy Canyon of Santa Barbara and Santa Ynez Valley— a region sporting more "Santas" than a New York shopping mall at Christmas.

The historical significance of the vineyards here is as rich in early California beginnings as Bordeaux's Old World roots run deep. Missions like San Borremo de Carmelo, Santa Clara, San Luis Obispo, Santa Cruz, Santa Ynez, San Juan Batista and Monterey were producing sacramental wines by the barrelfull; the vines sharing the same piney breezes and maritime air those red cheeked Friars experienced back in the day.

The establishment of these missions along the Central Coast provided more than mere places of worship, they also attended to the soldier and traveller with food and lodging. To meet service and labor needs the church enslaved local Native Americans. They worked the the mission farms, produced bricks for structures, made saddles and soap for Spanish soldiers, and worked the mission grounds– planting, pruning, picking, and stomping the mission grapes. Perched on elevated platforms, entire Native American families would crush the grapes as the juice drained down into cowhide bags.

The Missionaries who established vast acreage for their own, unknowingly became part of a monumental wine growing region– embraced by wine enthusiasts from around the world. Today nothing resonates with the wine industry's mounting success more than the Central Coast. Due to its vast plantable acreage and fitting terroir, vineyards are thriving and the region is scoring big.

Driving towards the center of the region, passing the vast row crops so abundant in the Salinas Valley, I could see the Santa Lucia Highland vineyards in the distance; the terraced bench land and hillsides rising in elevation to a height of approximately 1200 feet. In order to taste the acclaimed wines from here, one has to drive over these mountains to Carmel Valley. It's a different vibe tasting wines from a land not surrounded by vineyards of its own. Yet it's becoming the way to go for many wineries, some even establishing their tasting rooms in major cities.

I was best able to understand this "remote tasting room" success while visiting with former cattle rancher turned farmer John Boekenoogen. We met at his tasting room in the heart of the Carmel Valley tourist district.

John comes from a long line of cattlemen who have lived in the Santa Lucia Highland region for generations. He never had any intentions of planting vineyards until the day a buyer showed up on his mountain property and wanted to pay "good money" for a chunk of land. Flags flew. He told this prospective buyer "the land isn't for sale."

And why the interest?

Sure, from the mountain tops it's a great view of the Salinas Valley where rows of broccoli and thirty shades of lettuce poke their leafy heads out of the ground. But who wants to pay big money for a panoramic view of vegetables? Not to mention the afternoon winds that blow through. If I pay for land I want a coastal view– not a view of the "worlds largest salad bowl" as John refers to it.

So John questioned the interest these buyers had and discovered that his southeast facing land consisting of gravelly, sandy loam was ideal country for something more than cattle– of all things, vineyards.

After some negotiations with the buyers they came to terms. They were allowed to plant, but not to buy. And for ten years John sourced his grapes with one stipulation: if he were to build a winery he would be allowed to use his own grapes.

The rest was history as his family followed the winemaking call. Boekenoogen built a winery and his son Garret eventually became winemaker. His daughter Kate continues to work on the ranch and in the winery, while his second daughter Holly is involved with marketing the Boekenoogen label.

John speaks fondly of his years cattle ranching and row crop farming, though his heart now is in his winemaking. While reflecting on those days he said, "You can take a head of lettuce, hold it in your hand and say 'Hey, check this out.' But it's a head of lettuce. Hold up a glass of wine and you've got something."

This "something" resonates with those who appreciate Santa Lucia Highland wines. The Santa Lucia Highland AVA was established in 1991 and stretches along twelve miles of bench land. John pulled out the AVA map and pointed to the region's distinct geography. Due to Monterey Bay's south-east air flow funneling through the mountain pass, the vineyards here are recipients of cool mornings and sunny afternoons, allowing for a lengthy growing season.

As John looked with admiration at the crowd filling this off site tasting room, I understood that successful marketing delivers where the people are. In this case beautiful Carmel Valley.

John Boekenoogen has created a legacy here. It hasn't been easy. He makes it clear the business of wine comes with hard work and many challenges– no one better understands the wrangling it takes to get here than this man.

Recently a land with few vineyards, the region now boasts approximately 6,000 planted acres producing world class wine– this due to the grit and hard work by growers like John. He's proud of his success and it shows. "Of course," he says with a telling smile, "you're only as good as your last vintage."

And while each vintage will inevitably have its own set of challenges, the regions themselves continue marching forward. Take Paso Robles, whose 700,000 total acres of land is a Central Coast behemoth. Its footprint is Susquatchen, with 32,000 planted acres and growing– this while consistently producing wines of acclaim.

One man renowned for his contributions to Paso Robles' success in the business of wine is Gary Eberle, considered the "Godfather" of the AVA. Gary was not only the first wine grower to plant Cabernet Sauvignon in the region and the first to introduce Syrah into the country, he also helped champion the designation of Paso Robles as an AVA in 1983.

I had the privilege to sit with Gary at his winery overlooking a block of estate Cabernet Sauvignon and Mill Road Viognier. Gary talked about the winery's beginnings. It was evident his passion with wine runs deep. And I'm not just referring to the 17,000 square feet of underground caves he's built– another first for the region– the wines

produced by Eberle are reaching acclaim.

And while this former Penn State defensive lineman, who played for Joe Paterno, speaks of the region's wine scoring success, he doesn't sugar coat it. There are some hard hitting challenges like disease and water regulations that impact the bottom line. "Remember," Gary says, "this is an industry that prides itself on breaking even."

Of course being the "godfather" of the region and in the company of men like Dick Peterson, Robert Mondavi, and Daryl Corti, there's good reason to believe Gary, along with his wife Marcy, are achieving far greater than "breaking even." Their accomplishments clearly attest to this.

Yet beyond Eberle's accolades or any number of wine scorings, there is a humbleness to his demeanor. There is a profound sense of comfort that resonates with Gary at his vineyard home. Maybe it's being couched on his sixty-five acre estate, surrounded by land he's worked and cared for since the early seventies, that allows him to feel so at rest.

Although one has to ask, when does he find time to rest? Grape growing is hard work. There's always something to tackle. And while he faces his challenges head on he exudes a sense of connection to the land that speaks of a kinder, more gentle man– not a linebacker knocking helmets on the turf. The more he spoke of caring for his vineyards and tending to the cork oak on the property, the more I understood what was going on. This is not merely a business to Eberle. The land and the vineyards transcend personal value and reach further than his achievements.

PASO ROBLES

— AMERICAN VITICULTURAL AREA —

As he continued talking about what the land meant to him, to his family, to his employees and to the community, he was momentarily interrupted— turning to the vineyards he said:

"I will die on this property."

The words caught me off guard. It took a moment to actually understand where he was coming from. The fact that they were even spoken during this meeting may have been awkward for some, it wasn't for me. His words were unguarded and genuine. They resonated with what this "property" honestly meant to this gentleman farmer and accomplished wine grower. It was in every way the ultimate nod to the idea that place really does matter. Not just what elements are found in its dirt or what next year's change in climate might bring, but how the land is connected to the very backbone of Eberle himself.

Here was the heart and soul of a man who wasn't leaving. This was home. Home for his wife Marcy, their two standard poodles Sangio J and Rousainne, and home to those who worked here— they're all family— all part of a sustainable connection to "place." Where else in all the world could things matter more to so passionate a man than his vineyard home?

The days ahead of Eberle appear far more modest than most pioneers in the wine industry. "My

"Here was the heart and soul of a man who wasn't leaving....
Where else in all the world could things matter to so
passionate a man than his vineyard home?"

dream of retiring is to simply pull up a chair at the tasting room entrance," he says. That's it. To greet those coming to taste his award winning wines.

I couldn't help but be impressed by this man whose aspirations have helped him climb the mountain of success– where the air may be thin, but there's no need for oxygen. Not up here. The land is what he lives and breathes.

He has only to "pull up the chair."

Just a short poke up the road from Eberle winery there's an old stagecoach stop. After over one hundred years it's now the Tobin James winery and tasting room.

There's a promise here that the American west still lives. Pushing through the front doors you'll find everything to kick up your preceptors. Great taste and an excellent staff graciously serving wine from behind three western style back bars. The oldest bar was built in 1860 and came straight from Missouri.

The crowd noise carries out the front doors on almost any given day. It's not the noise of cowpokes, rough riders or gunslingers dropping in for a snort– they'll be no hold ups other than a line of purchasing guests at the cash register; it's of a crowd, or posse, taking in the vibe you get the moment you push through the front door– that feeling one experiences when removed from daily life.

I had this feeling while sitting with Claire and Lance Silver on their old west style balcony above the tasting room. It was in 1996 when they partnered with Tobey James to become co-owners of the winery established in 1993. They never looked back. Their loyal followers which include a massive number of club members, perhaps the biggest in the world, is astonishing. "We have 30,000 club members," Claire states. Lance nodding that it's true. He doesn't add puffery to these numbers but will remind you, "This is without a marketing staff."

And that's big. Claire points out that "our club members are our sales staff." This should explain a thing or two about loyalty to their wines. Apparently club members posse up to get the word out and it's working. At the forefront of this massive host of members are the challenges of taking care of them. To do so they've got to have award winning wines and hospitality that is second to none– not to mention a shipping staff with an Amazon sized record of delivery success.

Belly up to one of their bars and you'll experience the extent of this hospitality. Personalities are found in the glass with wines like James Gang Chardonnay, Fatboy Zinfandel and Blue Moon Reserve Syrah– just a few of the fine wines you'll meet here. The signature Tobin James Winery Starburst icon sets the stage for a star filled experience, and their jingle "Paso Robles in a glass" speaks of the depth of their wines– the importance this region has in terms of making it big.

Before leaving the Paso Robles region there's a place nearby called San Simeon Castle. It is perched like most ocean facing properties with breathtaking views, only this one's larger. Of course we're talking about the humble abode built by former icon publishing magnate William Randolph Hearst.

Situated within the Central Coast AVA, the castle was built in 1919 and stands today as a California Historical Landmark. I know it affords pleasure to many, but I'm not one for being herded onto buses or trailing sheeplike while being serenaded by expert tour guides– it's just not my thing– but I took the tour. The opportunity to see this California magnate's over the top crib was too much to pass. So as the former cattleman Boekenoogen would say, "I bit the bullet." I took the tour.

I've learned a great deal since that tour. Not only about Hearst's wealth or media empire, but about his interest in wine– it was his taste for comfort that intrigued me. It's rumored he spoke to his architect Julia Morgan about being tired of going "up there" and sleeping in tents on his property. "I'm getting a little too old for that. I would like to get something a little more comfortable," he is quoted as saying. Right? He wanted something more comfortable than a tent, so apparently he got to thinking, why not build some walls and garner them with ancient Church parts and tapestries from around the world. Maybe rather than dipping his toe into the seasonal brook he could have an Olympic Swimming pool to do cannon balls in. Rather than those awkward fold up chairs, why not some pillowy furniture from Henry the 8th, or whatever. Oh, and those canvas army cots he slept on–

not for me. Let's maybe get Napolean's bed and marbled stone shower rooms from King Tut's tomb. Perfect!

But wait, better yet Julia... let's just make it a castle. One with a wine cellar fully stocked. This might be an appropriate substitute for a Coleman camping cooler.

It is recorded that the wine cellar was constructed and stocked with few California wines. Hearst favored French and German. In fact, he served wines at his dinner parties during prohibition. He believed "temperance" should be practiced but scoffed at prohibition. In 1929 he wrote, "I consider the 18th amendment not only the most flagrant violation of the basic American principle of personal liberty that has ever been imposed on the American public, but the most complete failure as a temperance measure that has ever been conceived and put into impractical operation."

Hearst insisted on vaulted steel doors to guard his wine cellar during prohibition. Few knew he had this cellar, and that the keys to it were kept in his front pocket. And what raiding Fed in his right mind would insist Hearst empty his pants pockets!

Further south beyond Hearst's San Simeon Castle is Edna Valley, a sub-appellation with 22,500 total acres and 3500 acres of planted vineyards. There is a story evolving here. One beyond the prominent acres of Chardonnay and Pinot Noir varietals so esteemed by wine growers throughout this cool climate region. It's the rise of Rhône– an eminent contender in the business of Edna Valley wine. Rhône varietals are finding love among the region's rippling hills and volcanic soil. And no more a man to champion the cause than Rhône Valley pioneer himself, John Alban.

Just in from the Hospice Du Rhône International, he must have been exhausted– he didn't show it. As we entered his office he made it clear, "You'll find more than you need to know about me on the internet," he says without blinking. "Why are you here?"

"I want to tell your story" I replied. "No," he said pointedly, "you want to tell your story. Mine's all on the Internet."

Fair enough.

But it wasn't the Internet I wanted to shake hands with. It wasn't about tapping with my fingers what a million Googlers had already done– searching and finding something significant about the man on the screen. That was the Internet's story. I wanted John Alban's. I wanted to meet the Rhône Ranger himself. Though I never expected to be put front and center with a fully loaded, trigger happy scholar hung over from a weekend of hard work.

Later I came to understand that this was a man selflessly willing to give of his time, while careful not to waste it. And while John gave generously of his time– it was more than he first had to offer. His carefully guarded references to Edna Valley and his grape growing neighbors and people in the

business was genuine and respectful. It was something flat screens just can't convey. When addressing industry issues like terroir, appellations and varietals, he would unleash a vocabulary based on experience most text books couldn't keep up with. No stumbling, no contradicting. I was wondering if there was a John Alban App I should've downloaded before the interview.

I sat in the chair thinking, where in the hell did this guy come from? Seriously. I wanted a bottle of Alban wine just because he was drinking it. Syrah? Hell ya! Pour me a glass. Grenache? Voignier? I'll take a case of that. And I really had no idea whether his wines were as acclaimed as his accolades claimed them to be. The fact is I didn't care. I just wanted to be drinking what this guy was.

What John Alban has accomplished during his affair with Rhône Valley wines is unprecedented. Alban Winery is "the first American winery and vineyard established exclusively for Rhône varietals." That's big. At his 250 acre estate there are around 60 planted acres of vineyards— all Rhône vari-etals. The region's average 330 foot elevation may not be high, but his consistent 90 something Parker scores are. Alban's Syrah and Viognier reflect the importance of why fit matters. He speaks of the importance of terroir first— to those varietals perfectly tailored to this place he calls home.

There is no embellishing his accomplishments. He is in every way an icon. But he will at every turn take you away from that— to not allow you to focus on himself. There is a mystery to John, something pleasantly guarded and alluring. It's not about his Arron Eckhart looks, nor the shit detector constantly blinking in the back of his mind. It's about a similar character reminiscent in his wines— those dark and complex wines he has pioneered since 1989.

"He speaks of the importance of terroir first– to those varietals perfectly tailored to this place he calls home."

And while California continues to celebrate the grand Bordeauxs and Burgundies of the region, Alban is tirelessly working to further his affair with the increased popularity of Rhône varietals— those the New World has for decades referred to as insignificant or forgotten.

When I asked John about being an icon in the business he poo-pooed the idea. "What really defines an icon?" he asked.

Once again directing attention away from himself. So with that, I indulged. For a wine industry icon like Alban it's obviously more than a symbol— more than a smiley face or tiny screen symbol we tap with our finger tip; more than a Nike swoosh or a McDonald's arch.

In Alban's case an icon is one's contribution to a subject. It is an individual who breathes greater life into a matter the world is enhanced by. There is a global promise embedded in an icon. It is a promise that one's work will not be forgotten. There is no embellishing it. It takes rare perseverance and greater commitment. One does not follow without the other.

Ultimately an icon is a standard by which the end of the tape defines the length of its measure. The greater the measure the further the achievement– the more pronounced is the icon. Within the wine industry there are icons like Mondavi, Gallo, and Tchelistcheff, all measured and defined by their achievements.

What has been pioneered with Rhône varietals in Edna Valley will be addressed for decades to come. It is a single legacy of a forgotten and little cared for varietal left at the back of the room. Today, due to Albans perseverance, Rhône Valley varietals have been allowed to come forward– no longer bullied or neglected– but now sitting at the front of the class providing answers to questions others once deemed insignificant.

With our visit coming to an end, John escorted me out the door. We walked into the foray between the crush pad and his office. As we stepped into the foray I noticed five oak doors in a circle. It was perplexing. The room was shaped curiously in the form of an enclosed wine vat... or something. And of course I opened the door and stepped into a darkened room.

"You're not the first to walk into that closet," John said. "We call this the Frank Loyd Wrong room." It was cause for a good laugh. As we continued our exit and entered the crush pad there was the familiar smell of wine in production along with the sense of camaraderie among those working there.

It smacked with the industry's best. Clearly, whatever John's doing outside of the foray he's doing it "Wright."

And you won't find that on the Internet.

What you will find nearby Edna Valley is a micro climate hidden in the upper Arroyo Grande Valley. It is a remote wine growing region called Saucelito Canyon. Located south of Lake Lopez, it is seated virtually in the palm of nowhere. There is a sense of place here that takes you back in time as it defines San Luis Obispo County's wine heritage.

And no one knows it better than Bill and Nancy Greenough. In 1974, Bill began resurrecting Saucelito Canyon's 3 acres of lost Zinfandel vineyards that had been planted in the 1880's. It now appears these vines have discovered the fountain of youth due to one man's care and ultimate perseverance. Along with his attention comes a sense of place that matters. Imbued within the soil is "subtle gravel" and alluvial deposits– a past ocean floor releasing nutrients essential to the vine. It is a rare orchestrated symphony of climate, soil, place and people that is producing the fine nuances present in the world class wines being produced here.

When Bill first heard of the neglected vineyard overcome by poison ivy and tangled shrubs, and being foraged on by grazing cattle, he became intrigued. So he camped out on the property. Life at that moment changed course

"It is a rare, orchestrated symphony of place and people producing world class wines, conducted by the Greenough family."

for Greenough. His life would soon be defined by the vines he slept with– an affair that would last to this day. There was a feeling here that resonated with Bill on more levels than even he seems to understand.

I sat with Bill on his rustic deck overlooking the ancient and flourishing vines. He spoke of the early days constructing the ranch house while bringing life back to the vineyard. The ranch house may be "off the grid" as he says, but it has been a place of family celebrations for decades. This is where he slept while rejuvenating the 3 acres of Zinfandel, and where he would later plant additional blocks of vineyards. Had it not been for Bill, there's a good chance these old vines would not be here today.

Yet some credit to their survival should be shared with a man named Henry Ditmas. It is beyond thinking that in the 1880's this Englishman would chose the right varietal fit at a time when varietals were instead chosen for their popularity.

There is a sense of viticultural appeal in these crowned old vines– a nobility to their presence. They appear to have been knighted by mother time; allowed to pass by the wrath of rot and decay, disease and pestilence, to live another day. Here too, the mountains appear unchanged. In the distance, Hi Mountain still captures its ancient dreamy sunsets that appear on Saucelito Canyon Vineyard's label. The fossilized oysters, clams and silver dollars embedded along the local creek beds rest in their same places. These fossils dating back millions of years. So common are the over weighted crustaceans the Greenoughs use them throughout the ranch house as attractive doorstops.

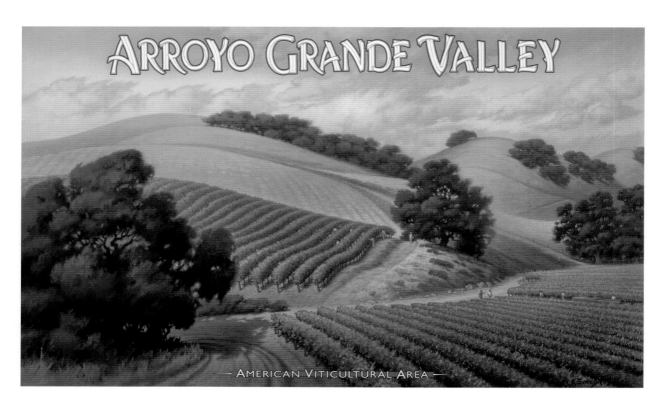

They speak of a distant time when the ocean lay over the land, and the stubbing of one's toe is a blunt reminder of their petrified existence.

As I walked the canyon flats and subtle hillsides, I better understood Bill's feelings as I contemplated its vineyard past. It is just the "eons ago" thing I shy away from. Attempting to wrap my mind around things as overwhelming or intense as how the land was formed is incomprehensible to me. It's like a math equation gone rogue. There are those professionals who know it best, but even they rely on a great amount of speculation. There is a sheer brightness to its power. I imagine Einstein's shabby hair catching fire at the very thought of it.

Personally, I prefer living in the present and that day was no exception. While the sun rose and the crows criss-crossed the vineyards— chatty in the morning light— I felt more alive. Simply because it was the promise of a new day. The first light, briefly overcoming the surrounding mountain tops then washing over rows of the old vines, filled the canyon to the brim with warmth. The paired doves in flight with their soft wings drumming, seemed to follow time as it moved along— as it has for eons— one sunrise at a time.

The old thriving vineyards have given thanks to this gentleman farmer. Beyond the sweat, the challenges, the consuming of his life, there was always a profound need to take care of something meaningful— a parallel in his own life. This one night stand became a business endeavor lasting Greenough to this day. And over time there had become only one way to approach it. That way is a perspective the Greenough's refer to as the "Saucelito Way." As unique a perspective ever embraced by a family paying homage to the synergies of "place." It has become a continuum of tradition based upon family values.

Bill and Nancy's son Tom is a second generation farmer and winemaker who embraces this "Saucelito Way." Bill is there to support and help guide his son when needed, while Nancy keeps the ship on course. Tom's own passion for the vines has overtaken his father's. I saw it first hand during my stay.

Behind a colossal live oak tree on the ranch, whose strapping limbs once supported the wooden water tank used for the Ditmas endeavors, was an earthen cellar. It was carved into the hillside beneath the oak tree's shadow, and had stored Ditmas wines all those years ago. It was here that I met Tom. He spoke about the land with life experiences beyond his years. He spoke of the future, about planting the nearby brushy hills with vines. I could not help but be impressed by his vision. The young man who's followed his father's path has himself caught the wine bug fever— this with a passion all his own.

And Tom's efforts are bringing acclaimed wines to the table; their 1880 Zinfandel having won numerous awards along with their Petite Syrah and Arroyo Grande Valley red blends.

While we talked casually outside beneath the Saucelito Canyon sun, our attention once again turned to the oak. Tom mentioned an arborist had dated the tree to be close to 300 years old; that "the oak tree spends 150 years of its life growing and another 150 years of its life dying." It was a profound

statement– that with every life there reaches a crescendo– a point when the ebbing of life begins to descend into the reflective pool of old age.

Yet here in Saucelito Canyon, where the old vineyards continue to thrive, time seems to have forgotten their presence. After over a hundred years the ebbing of this vineyard's life has clearly not begun. Perhaps its lengthy life is due to what's buried within its treasured soils, bundled with the Greenough's "Saucelito way"– a fine balance sustaining life. In this remote place "off the grid," where a sense of timelessness continues to breathe over the land, these vines continue to celebrate life.

Leaving the Greenough ranch was like leaving an old friend. But there were other regions to visit. As I travelled south the cooling Santa Maria Valley lay open to the west with its shinning stars... wineries like Cambria, Bien Nacido, Byron and others. Ahead was Solvang and Lompoc– two regions that have grown with leaps and bounds in the past few years.

Passing the many vineyards and open grasslands I soon came upon the quaint town of Los Olivos where wineries like Fess Parker and Firestone Vineyards adorn the town's fringes.

Before entering the heart of Los Olivos, I turned on a country road leading me through a mountain corridor that traversed a short grade to the west. The road twisted in elevation until it opened up to Ballard Canyon.

This was a place more reminiscent of

Sonoma County– my hometown. A place where oak trees grew large and seasonal creeks babbled until late spring, turning thirsty and dry into summer.

Here the canyons draw you in, welcoming you with hillsides couched in the most comfortable of settings. There is a shared communion between the acres of open grassland and vineyard presence. It's a pairing that compliments both the region's natural beauty and its inescapable charm.

> " ... a pairing that compliments both the region's natural beauty and its inescapable charm. "

Santa Barbara County has a jewel here in Ballard Canyon embracing each visitor with close to 8,000 planted acres and growing. It's a draw. The sub-appellation was established in 2013 and is relatively new. Its sand and limestone soils, inclusive of a canyon that runs north to south, is only a small measure of a larger vineyard equation. The Canyon is nestled between cooler Sta. Rita Hills AVA to the west and the more heated Happy Canyon of Santa Barbara AVA to the east. This micro climate with wind, sun and fog is strictly Ballard Canyon's own. The vineyards here consist mostly of Syrah and Sangiovese with smaller blocks of Merlot, Cabernet Franc and Sauvignon Blanc.

Located in the sweet spot of the alluring Santa Ynez Valley there are a host of vineyards like Beckman and Larner, yet there is only one winery with a single tasting room, a gorgeous setting, and immaculately cared for vineyards.

It is Rusack Winery and Vineyards. With 17 acres of planted grapes, attention to detail compliments the allure of these low lying hills. Exquisite rose bushes are planted before each row of vineyards adorning the entrance to the winery with perfect care. Rusack's promise to the visiting wine enthusiast is that taste really begins at the front door.

I had the pleasure of sitting with Rusack's winemaker Steven Gerbac beneath the canopy of a host of live oaks. It was outside the winery's tasting room overlooking a block of vineyards. He and several others, including Wes Hagen, championed the AVA designation. They drove the Ballard Canyon hilltops, defined the landmarks, and at the end of the day drew the plans and submitted them for federal designation.

Having first worked as assistant winemaker here, Gerbac's mastered the art of fine wine in the very appellation he's helped define. He's putting his years of experience and firm belief of the region's potential to good use. Like most winemakers he knows the vineyards, and while moving through the ranks of the Rusack venture, knows them well.

Of course having a tasting room attached to the winery, staked profusely within its own vineyards is a synergy that's working for both the Rusacks and Gerbac, along with throngs of wine enthusiasts seeking great taste. The wines, like the view, don't disappoint.

There is something surprisingly fresh about a winery whose estate has the ability to bottle and pour wines where their vineyards thrive. To taste the wines that come from the vineyard one is viewing is to experience the nuances brought to perfection in the glass. Its pairing is a presentation not found with off-site tasting.

The very essence enhancing wine is "place," and to be a part of that when drinking wines has relevance. Here, our preceptors breathe the same air, feel the same sun and look upon the very soils the vineyards thrive in. It is getting to know the wines from the inside out.

I understand the need to market where tourism has its draw. Satellite tasting rooms are the new thing for many wineries. It's business and it's working. But when you step onto the grounds of a winery like Rusack's— sit beneath the welcoming arms of shading oak trees while looking upon the vineyard whose wine you hold in your hand— there's a certain unalienable vibe to the experience. It's real and never disappointing.

Steven pointed towards vineyards once planted with grape varietals less appreciative of the Ballard Canyon climate. "The vineyards have been replaced by vines that are more conducive to the land," he says. It's become standard practice, one that every grower has embraced... plant what fits.

The following afternoon I met with Geoff Rusack. We sat beneath the same magnificent oaks overlooking the large crowds that once again had gathered to taste, laugh and relax. As we spoke

STA. RITA HILLS

— AMERICAN VITICULTURAL AREA —

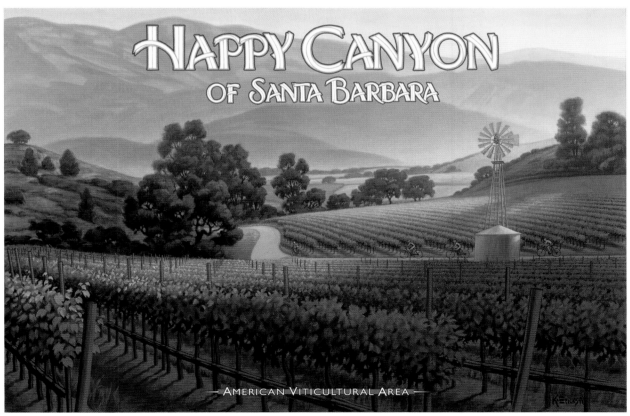

HAPPY CANYON
OF SANTA BARBARA

— AMERICAN VITICULTURAL AREA —

about Rusack Winery and his Santa Catalina Island endeavor I noticed Geoff's eyes wandering. He wasn't impressed by his grand achievements within the industry. While attentive to our conversation he appeared infatuated by the imbibing crowd. It was a telling moment. His subtle smile revealed what matters deeply to those who care about this business of wine. Beyond the financial goals or responsibilities, there comes a great sense of satisfaction derived by pleasing others. Rusack wasn't a conglomerate executive grinning about wine sales or stock prices. There were no "cha- chings" sounding off in the back of his head as he watched the wine crowd drink it in. Rusack was pleased because they were. He, like the many men and women working in the wine business, have a distinct love affair with people. After all, this is a business rooted in the world of hospitality.

And while Geoff was clearly humbled by the sight of the crowd he was vicariously sharing in their celebration. The moment helped me better understand this complex business of wine and its human connection. The personality, character and nuances that define the best of wine, define as well the best of individuals– the men and women whose monumental contributions to the bottle go unseen.

THE SOUTH COAST
American Viticultural Area

Comedian Fred Allen once said, Southern California's "a fine place to live, if you happen to be an orange." That was then. Today it might be said the South Coast is a fine place to live if you happen to be a grape– or more fittingly, married among them.

This isn't due to the region morphing into a grape growing Mecca. It's about wineries scoring big with wedding venues, barrel room parties and posh event centers. Wineries have become a happening place in the South Coast. They are benefited by the fact that profit margins are no longer simply based on drinkability, but also the successful marketing of these important events– this padding pocketbooks and keeping many out of the red. And with the region's proximity to a colossal population, it's a big "Oh, hell ya!" for every winery.

Yet, before the population boom, concrete channels, toll roads and the Kardashians, Southern California was a land defined by its agriculture. The warm climate influenced people to relocate in droves from across the country, settling among its mouth watering citrus groves. It was a renaissance led by an aggressive turn of the century travel campaign, marketing what the finest wines define best: "sense of place." This was not only about living comfortably, but let's face it, about living fat.

The allure was undeniable. Agriculture was huge. Its business opportunities were exploding. Aircraft makers like Douglas, Hughes and Lockheed eventually headquartered here. Hollywood brought industry and celebrity to the state as it continued to grow– not just massive egos, but concrete blocks and plump, juicy fruit.

The South Coast continues to be a branded paradise. Even today's vineyards are finding some love on the outskirts of the thriving and towering steel metropolis. Among the unincorporated hillsides and valleys void of concrete structures are scattered 3000 acres of planted vineyards. The region's heavy air, ocean influence, well draining soil and sun speak of a region not only home to today's massive infrastructure but one suited to vineyards. Varietals like Cabernet Sauvignon, Chardonnay, Zinfandel, and Sauvignon Blanc are thriving among their neighboring urban digs.

The South Coast AVA was established in 1985 and includes five counties: Los Angeles, Riverside, San Bernadino, San Diego and Orange County. With an AVA population of approximately

20 million, it's colossal. Temecula Valley, Ramona Valley, and San Pasqual Valley are among the South Coast's sub-appellations.

Along Temecula's Rancho California road where Franciscan priests once traveled is where sacramental wines of the mid 1700's brought the first vines to the region; and the 1960's brought the boom— a renaissance that kickstarted Temecula Valley's flourishing grape growing region.

Today Temecula Valley is the region's largest wine producer— home to almost 1300 acres of planted vineyards, where cooling breezes from the neighboring ocean and some serious heat from the east is bringing life to the region's signature varietals. The vineyards are benefited by low coastal passes like Rainbow Gap and Temecula Gorge that open and reach inland. The heavy ocean air is drawn inland due to rising warm air from the east.

When you hear the name Temecula or "Temecunga," as the Luiseno Indian once eloquently referred to as "place of sun," there remains an indigenous romance to this sub-appellation. Today the region is not only about its wines, but for many it's about the "road trip" to the AVA's most undisputed wine country party draw. From Los Angeles, Riverside, San Diego and beyond, the hipsters, baby boomers, millennials, young and old, are drawn to the region from their nearby digs. They come to indulge in the region's abundant play zone as much as they come to taste. Take Temecula's *New Year's Grape Drop* that attracts a sizable crowd, or the flaming balloons lifting people high above the vineyards. There is also the *Wild Women of the Wine Country 5K* hosted by Wein Family

Cellars and Ponte Vineyards. Personally, I'm waiting for the first winery to sponsor sleepovers among the vineyards.

The first commercial winery was established in Temecula by golf icon Eli Callaway Jr. whose vineyard plantings began in 1969. The region has grown immensely since Calloway's first endeavor. Due to his success Temecula made headlines when Queen Elizabeth the II and his Royal Highness partook in two glasses of Calloway's 1974 White Riesling at a luncheon in New York. The Queen requested to meet the vintner and gentleman farmer. Nothing like a hole in one for Ely Calloway Jr.'s early wine endeavor.

After Calloway sold the winery to conglomerate Hiram Walker & Sons in 1981 he went on to make another hole in one with the creation of Big Bertha— a monster headed club that would become a golf industry sensation.

Though Temecula speaks of a 60's renaissance, it is the Cucamonga Valley in San Bernadino County that is recorded to have the greatest grape growing history. Early endeavors began in 1838 with Tribucio Tapia at his Cucamonga Rancho. Here is where the region's vineyards and dry farming has its roots. As the region grew, it was the early pioneer grower Secundo Fillipi who boasted it to be the largest grape growing region in the world— recorded to have planted more than 20,000 acres— this prior to prohibition. It was Secundo Fillipi who founded the Italian Vineyard Company (IVC) in 1883 and brought the first massive wine production to the Cucamunga Valley. The fourth generation of Fillip farmers have been instrumental in establishing the 1995 Cucamunga Valley AVA that today has approximately 1000 planted acres.

Unfortunately, infrastructure is gaining the most traction in the region. Its concrete, steel, and massive pavement is far more favorable than growing vineyards. The necessary four lane freeways are a place where you get to know your neighbor's bumper well.

Beyond the land gulping metropolis of Los Angeles' South Coast AVA is the most recent Malibu Coast AVA. Though not part of the South Coast AVA, it is a neighboring region beginning nearby the Pacific Coast Highway. Here, the few blocks of seaside vineyards begin their climb high above Malibu's extensive rooftops– reaching for the higher elevated Newton Canyon and Saddle Rock sub-appellations.

In Malibu Coast, smaller vineyard blocks are most common. They adorn the dry steepened landscape where growers like Gabrielle Harris of Sage Hill Vineyards is bringing acclaim to the region. Her 2013 Syrah/Cabernet Sauvignon blend won a bronze and her 2010 Syrah made "special mention" in the prestigious 2015 International Decanter Awards. I had the pleasure of visiting with owner grower Gabrielle Harris at her quaint vineyards rooted among the steep Santa Monica Hills. She was delighted to have "the first Malibu wine to win this international competition." This with 15,000 entries.

And she's not alone in her success. Today Malibu Coast AVA has over fifty vineyards throughout the region with others achieving

recognition themselves. Many individuals with past business endeavors have moved on to grape growing. They are financially secure. They've come to know the value of life among vineyards and the quality of wines that can be produced here, as well as the challenges that come with them.

With present laws not permitting wineries to exist in the Malibu Coast region, growers have adopted assistance from co-op facilities like the nearby custom crush in Camarillo– allowing local growers to produce their own wine with in-house winemakers who understand the craft.

At this time there are 210 acres of vineyards planted in the Malibu appellation and nearly 50 commercial wine grape growers– with not one winery to call their own. Of those planted acres varietals like Cabernet Sauvignon and Merlot grow in the higher elevations, while varietals like Pinot Noir and Chardonnay grow nearer the coastline. Syrah, Malbec, Sauvignon Blanc and many other varietals are also calling Malibu their home– half to seven acres of planted vineyards is most common.

Though vineyard planting has transcended upon this peaceful land and has settled in beautifully, obstacles and challenges are threatening its future.

One significant challenge confronting growers is a new era of prohibition threatening the Malibu Coast. It's not about banning wine production as in the past– an era that leveled the industry– it's about today's prohibition with vineyard planting, That's right. It's about putting a halt to vineyards– the very attraction both traveler and wine enthusiast appreciate;

the green undulating rows that charm and dress the hillsides.

With some Los Angeles Supervisors it's become an "anything but vineyards."

"The good news is many wine growing regions like Malibu appear far more sustainable than the regulations governing them."

The good news is many wine growing regions like Malibu appear far more sustainable than the regulations governing them. Vineyards are historically passed on within the family; generations in touch with the land. I've see it throughout the state— a continuum of place and people while the changing landscape of state and federal regulations come and go. Planners, supervisors and politicians move on. Laws are amended.

And no one better champions the right for vineyards than Malibu Coast's own PR man, Dan Fredman. Fredman was hired by AVA president John Gooden to market the region. Fredman took me on a personal tour of this newest South Coast AVA. The attractive blocks of vineyards on dry, scrub brushed hillsides and canyon flats appeared to bring renewed life to the region.

As we ventured off the narrowing grades Fredman eventually ended the tour at PCH near the ocean. He pointed towards a stretch of Malibu beach. "Right there. That's Billionaire Beach." It smacked with an exclusive lifestyle— it spoke to me. Not of breaking waves but of beaches the public might never

have the opportunity to experience. For over two decades an easement had been blocked to the beach by wealthy landowners— the natural beauty of Billionaire Beach (Carbon Canyon Beach) was a California treasure not being shared. The wealthy felt themselves entitled to call it their own, to keep what was not theirs from others. They wanted privacy, and privacy is understandable— we all want views without public faces glaring at us. But the California Coastal Commission has guidelines the rich and famous ignored. Only, the people who came to use the beach didn't care about these home owners. The stars they were interested in came out at night— reflecting upon the great waters of the Pacific; not a paparazzi moment or a glance at some celebrity mug from a distance. For these tireless souls facing the wrong brought on by a privileged few, gaining access had become a challenge. And by digging in they got it done. The right to use land that was justly theirs was finally opened for all to share.

It is this sharing, this win, that is significant to the grape growers of the Malibu Coast today. The Billionaire Beach issue is a reflection of Malibu AVA's own restrictions. There is mounting frustration regarding local regulations that are hampering use of the land they own— regulations not allowing growers to plant vineyards on their own property; land they share by inviting the public in to taste, wander, and simply indulge in the beauty of Malibu itself. This is what wineries are historically known for— their hospitality and deliciousness.

Malibu Coast screams with, "Plant me your best!"

Yet, by not allowing wineries in Malibu and

limiting tasting rooms in the Malibu county hills, the LUP (Land Use Permit) restrictions hamper public access to some of Malibu's most charming hillside vistas— naturally beautiful places to relax at the table, to eat and drink. Fortunately, you can thank grape growers like John Gooden who continues to champion the Malibu Coast AVA.

I visited John and his wife De De at their Montage vineyard and home in Malibu. John pointed to the outdoor table where the makers of the Malibu AVA had sat and drafted the application. "It all began right there, at that table," he said admiringly.   And if you understood the paramount efforts involved in getting an AVA designation, you would understand the time spent at that table— drafting notes, due diligence, historical research, finding words to support the region's beautiful terroir with the most fitting varietals. It was more than a challenge, more than financially draining... it was daunting. Fortunately the growers are doers. They understand markets. They appreciate taste. And they were passionate about bringing the AVA to fruition because they knew the quality of the grapes born from this unique land are exceptional.

We walked through Gooden's small terraced block of vineyards below their house. It was late February. Bud break was happening. De De, who is also a partner in the endeavor said, "We had a good rain that was followed by heat." This attributing to its spring-like burst of green bud and leafing.

"Vines need a consistent period of cold weather in the mid fifties to become rested," said John. And the region is noted for its short dormancy. If bud break comes too early it may lead to a host of

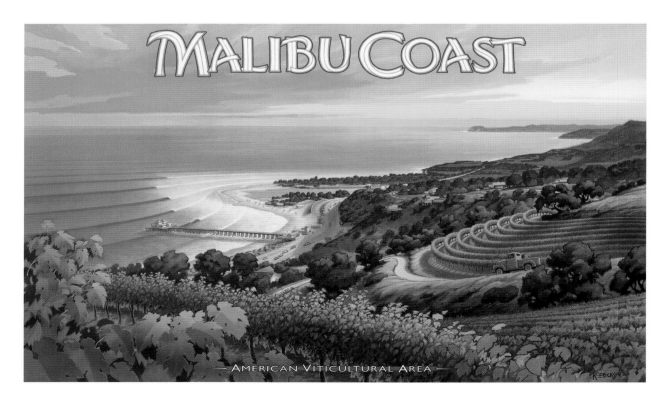

"His words resonated with the essence of why wine matters. It's about more than just drinkability. It's about relationships."

serious issues; mainly frost that can attack the frail bud and destroy an entire season's yield.

Later in the day we took a drive to a neighboring block of vineyards. It was a magnificent estate that Gooden helps manage, and not for any reason but because he wants to. It's also within Malibu city limits. We stood on a steepened hillside beside a block of Chardonnay, overlooking the ocean in the shadow of a healthy sycamore tree. As John reflected on the bud breaking vines he brought to mind what is commonly valued here...

"We're family owned. Everyone."

His words resonated with the essence of why wine matters. It's about more than just drinkability. It's about relationships. Growing grapes is as much a family affair with growers as cooking is in the kitchen. It's about being together and helping one another. It's about making something special.

While Malibu may be perceived by many as dripping with money and having buttery notes of coastal bliss, there's more to this legendary "endless summer" charm than a place to spend and surf. Its resources are reflected in the wine and in the uniqueness of the land– defined by a federally approved American Viticultural Area.

Malibu Coast also has its larger wine growers

like Cielo and Semler's Malibu Family wines, who have led the charge in the region. Semler's ranch, once an avocado farm in the 70's, was lost in a ravaging frost. Today there are vineyards, a zoo safari, and with good fortune a winery in the making.

I met with with Dakota Semler at their tasting room. He took me on a drive through the Malibu Family Wines estate vineyards. Rather than traveling among the vineyards in the customary ranch truck, we traversed the property in a zebra striped Tesla. It wasn't your ordinary sedan. Of course, this wasn't your ordinary vineyard either. When we entered the heart of the vineyards there were barking zebras, water buffalo and Stanley the giraffe from the movie *Hangover 3*. It seemed a fitting ride. Technology had come to the wineries. Whether by iPad, cellar innovations, weather alarms, or in this case a custom Tesla, tech gadgetry was evolving no less than the wines themselves have over the years.

To visit Semler is to know something's happening. It's more than technology, more than the adventure. The Semler's provide a visual wine tour like few others, and with 2000 visitors over the weekends indulging in its safari tour and open air tasting room, it's become a hip way to indulge. But it's not only about Stanley the giraffe peering over the fence posts. It's about the wine. Quality grapes. Varietals thriving in a land that's producing wines that are scoring big.

Dakota pulled alongside the vineyard road. With the sound of a "hee-hawing" Zebra in the distance, we stepped out for a short walk with a view of the fertile valley opening beneath Turtle and Saddle Rock. This was a land rich with Chumash legend and noted history. Within Turtle Rock caves are Petroglyphs a rock's throw away from the vineyards— an indigenous bit of Native American history in the heart of their grape growing.

I asked Dakota what led him to this wine country endeavor. He told me that prior to stepping knee deep into the wine industry, he had thoughts of becoming a commercial underwriter. There was good money in it. But "on a wine trip to the Mediterranean" he said his father took him aside... "Do you want to work a hundred hours a week at a job doing what you don't love? Or work in the vineyards that you do?" It was a seminal moment for Dakota whose passion for carrying on the legacy is today both intimate and revealing. And he has never looked back. He speaks of the vines that are thriving. He talks of the history and the joy of being a part of the vineyard— this sense of "every-whereness." It was remarkable, not because of the buzz associated with the industry, but the history— the continuum of family.

To understand Dakota Semler's decision is to know he is a part of something larger than himself. He is part of a family that began its journey with avocado farming and is now host to an animal sanctuary and a vineyard with acclaim.

Even Stanley the giraffe is feeling the love.

Another legacy in the works is Richard Hirsh's Cielo Vineyards. Here the "sense of place" resonates from within. The stone taken from his property was used in the construction of the tasting room walls.

I had the pleasure of tasting a delicious Woodstock labeled Cabernet Sauvignon blend with Richard and John Gooden. We sat at a lengthy rustic table within the tasting room's heavy stone walls.

Hirsh explained how The Woodstock label reflects the essence of the iconic music festival at Max Yagur's 600 acre dairy farm— a "cultural touchstone," one that crossed borders of race and the establishment. It was a moment of monumental peace, music and togetherness. The Cielo label is a tribute to that moment— reflective of the open love the era spoke of, and what wine itself reflects.

While tasting, Gooden says reverently, "I remember the day I was at Woodstock." This experience was a touchstone in his own life. It wasn't surprising. I think we all have been "there" in one way or another. John was one of the fortunate to have lived it.

Hirsh has created his own place here on the mountain top above the Malibu Coast— both breathtaking and reflective of the peace, beauty and spiritual culture his label represents. The costs involved with building a winery and tasting room of this significance can be monumental. Yet, most of these owner growers have made their dough. They understand with vineyard farming the financial callouses brought on by hard work are immense, that weather worries and regional dormancy issues will knowingly hound them. But "rolling up your sleeves" is in their blood. It's a community with a history of wealth born by fortitude, that is neither flaunted or abused, but healthy and sustainable. Ironically, while the growers' lifestyles smack with good living, it was pointed out to me by Dan Fredman that "there are more rehab centers allowed in Malibu than tasting rooms."

It's no revelation celebrities and those with financial wealth have chosen Malibu as home, or for those struggling, a place to recover. They are passionate about healthier living and creating a better lifestyle.

For the grape growers in Malibu, it's about less regulation. This allowing them to plant vineyards that may not be indigenous to the land, but that do speak of man's communion with it. This in itself is a beautiful thing— a matter of relevance. Scattered are the native pines, sycamore and scrub oak. The buck brush, chemise, and choking thickets bask in the ocean's reflective light and heat— soothed by maritime breezes. The vineyards themselves adorning this indigenous landscape with stitchings of green in summer and patterned colors in fall.

This natural beauty is captured at different twists and turns as you drive Muhlholland, Kenan, Point Dume, or Latigo Canyon and along the Pacific coastline. The turning roads lead you in... they take you down and lift you up. Like elegant drapery, vineyards adorn the harshness of their surroundings, gently humanizing the region's esthetic charm.

These vineyards are rooted in the signature

terroir— climate, minerals, elevation, the rain that falls and drought years that follow. It is what makes Malibu wine its very own. Each region embodies the essence of the land's personality. What other drink speaks so reverently of the land's natural indigenous character than wine?

"What other drink speaks so reverently of the land's natural indigenous character than wine?"

Not too distant from the Malibu Coast, beyond the curling set of waves lapping at its legendary shores, is California's most celebrated South Coast island, Catalina— located approximately twenty something miles across the gentle and tumultuous blue Pacific waters. Though not a designated AVA, the island's vineyard presence has a visceral sense of place unlike any other in the region, or for that matter, throughout the state.

Here, on Catalina Island, Geoff Rusack and his wife Alison Wrigley Rusack (heir to Wrigley Gum fortune) are daring to dream big. Their six acres of island planted vineyards may appear small, but the challenges are many.

I had the privilege of touring the island with Geoff Rusack. We left the quaint harbor town of Avalon on a clear sunny morning to visit their 85 year old El Rancho Escondido— a magnificent Spanish style mountain retreat and former iconic horse ranch. Of course this visit wasn't about equestrian matters, it was about viticulture. Specifically the idea of transforming an iconic 1500 acre Arabian horse ranch into a tasting room and world class winery— this being the first and only

> "On Catalina island, the vines are more vulnerable as the harsh maritime elements are coming at the vineyards from all sides."

commercial wine venture on a California island.

It was a spectacular morning with visibility as clear as the rich history of El Rancho Escondido– a time when Alison's parents, Helen and Phillip Wrigley, bred world class Arabians on their Catalina ranch.

Today, the transformation from horses to vineyards is a natural fit. It is also an extension born by a stable of delicious wines they produce at their iconic Ballard Canyon vineyards and winery in the Central Coast– only here on Catalina Island, the vines are more vulnerable as the harsh maritime elements are coming at the vineyards from all sides.

Yet, this hasn't deterred the Rusack's. Determined to grow island grapes and produce fine wines, in 2008 they planted 6 acres of vineyards at their El Rancho Escondido. The three varietals planted include Chardonnay, Pinot Noir, and Zinfandel.

Zinfandel is at the heart of the family's most recent story. When Rusack heard there were wild Zinfandel vines planted on neighboring Santa Cruz Island in the mid 1800's, it peeked an interest. So he, along with his two sons Austin and Parker, hiked the rugged terrain of Santa Cruz Island in search of the creeping vines. Successful in their efforts, Rusack had the clippings cloned. And by doing so, established a

continued history of Channel Island plantings.

Rusack's Central Coast viticulturist Larry Finkle believes the island has similar influences to the Russian River Valley appellation in Sonoma County. Yet there are many noticeable differences between the two distinct regions. One such difference is the treatment of deer fencing. While deer fencing is installed throughout many north coast regions, for Rusack's island vineyards it's a whole other story. Finkle has installed 2 and 3 inch steel posts to anchor the Rusack vineyard fencing. Sound like overkill? Sure, if not for the beastly bison grazing the open hog backs!

Brought over in 1924 for the *Vanishing America*, a movie based on Zane Grey's novel, the bison roam the island freely and are as fond of grapes as any creature with an appetite for taste– one that represents a cud chewing population in the state that is bigger than most.

In addition to bison, Catalina Island was once home to wild horses, grazing goats and tusk plowing boar that were eventually removed from the island due to their non indigenous presence. Black tail deer, foxes and other native animals continue to inhabit the island. But the bison have yet to be removed. It is said "they play an important role in the cultural fabric of the island." Maybe that's code for tourist attraction. Or maybe it's the Hollywood in them. Let's face it, they are

SANTA CATALINA ISLAND

— EL RANCHO ESCONDIDO —

celebrities and no one wants to knock a star— especially a heavy weight with a big head and sharp horns.

Unfortunately, I never did see a buffalo while on my travels. It wasn't really a bother, there was so much more to see. Especially with the day being strikingly clear and the mainland looking so remarkably close. "It is rare to see so far," said Rusack. In fact on his flight over to the island's "Airport in the Sky," it was the first time he could see all Channel Islands from the air at once.

And Rusack has seen a lot from the air. As a former aviation attorney his appreciation for air transport and planes was also very clear. While having coffee at the airport, he pointed out his sleek riveted Cessna Caravan 9 seater. He explained the large pod beneath its pregnant looking under belly was used to transport his cases of Catalina Island wine back to the island— wine from island sourced grapes that had been pressed, produced and bottled at the Rusack's Central Coast winery. The second Cessna Caravan in the family had its passenger seating removed and windows blacked out to provide care for the fresh picked fruit flown from the island to mainland winery.

After leaving the Airport we travelled further inland and soon arrived at the Arabian horse stables where the future tasting room and winery were presently under construction. Nearby were small blocks of dormant Pinot Noir, Chardonnay and his adventurously sought after Zinfandel vineyards, now managed by Finkle.

When speaking with Finkle it was clear— the challenges facing island grape growing are tremendous. "There are wasps, dust mildew, high magnesium and salt in the soil." Another element that can decimate a crop during "hang time" are the Santa Ana winds. The winds that originate from the mainland can blow north of 50 miles per hour. They're heated and intense, and when funneling from the east, gain speed and power before blowing through the island with ferocity. Rusack says these winds create "shatter" and at times may wreak havoc on a harvest.

I've anchored my own boat in Avalon harbor and have been tossed around by a severe Santa Ana wind storm. The sight of the crashing waves' foam kissing at the tops of the highest palm trees is stomach turning. Seagulls mostly don't fly; those which do, flop. Boats don't sail and moorings occasionally break loose. The potential damage these ferocious winds might do to an October harvest is frightening— and they blow in full force at peak of harvest.

This hasn't swayed the Rusacks. They welcome challenge. And with a built in market population of 20 million people across the San Pedro Channel, there appears to be no stopping what they can achieve. When I asked Rusack if he was going to expand his vineyards he said, "I have no plans to grow more." I sensed this could change. The Rusack's are "allowed a total of 18 acres to plant." There is much more to do.

As we returned to Avalon I better understood what was going on with Geoff and Alison's island endeavor. It was a continuum– one less associated with Chicago chewing gum, swinging baseball bats, or Arabian horses galloping across the Catalina headlands. Their journey was about reaching further and offering with their boutique stable of wines, a distinct character of their own. Their premium wines speak not only of a "place" out in the sea, but of an iconic family's roots growing deeper. Another generation tapping into the promise of something more than a continuing legacy or grand celebration of life, but the enhancing of its pleasures.